THE GUNS WE LEFT BEHIND

Tales of Culture and Caliber

P.R. Hirsh

BY P.R. HIRSH

Thanks for the SAKO 85!
Shopping in your store
reminds me of the
way gun sales used to be...
Classy!

For Anne, Forrest and Hunter

SPECIAL THANKS TO ERNEST COLSMANN OF COLSMANN ARMS IN MORGANTOWN, WV, AND MASTER GUNSMITH VINCENT CAPAN OF FAYETTE GUN SHOP IN FAIRCHANCE, PA.

VII

If

If you can keep your head when all about you
Are losing theirs and blaming it on you;
If you can trust yourself when all men doubt you,
But make allowance for their doubting too;
If you can wait and not be tired by waiting,
Or, being lied about, don't deal in lies,
Or, being hated, don't give way to hating,
And yet don't look too good, nor talk too wise

-First stanza of "IF" by Rudyard Kipling

CHAPTER 1

Guns in the Home

THE GUN WRITER

Morgantown, WV, 2014

Ladies and gentlemen, first and foremost, I want to stress that this is a book about people, not just firearms. The following stories reveal how culture and caliber intermix to create what some say is a dangerous and outmoded tradition. Perhaps, but there are more than three hundred million guns in public circulation and at least forty million gun owners who keep and bear them. In deference to the armed, it might be prudent to study just how deeply the gun theme runs from sea to shining sea.

Our nation is at an impasse over guns. On one side we have some pretty shook-up people who have endured a lifetime of negative messaging about guns. Average urbanites have no experience with gun culture. Certainly their reactions to gun violence are sincere and logical. Their emotion is honest and compassionate. Everybody in the neighborhood says the same thing: "It's a no-brainer. Ban anything that can cause a news story."

On the other side, we have a vast and largely misunderstood gun culture whose proverbial spokesperson would reply, "You have nooooo idea what you are asking."

This work is not designed to "sell anyone" on guns or gun control. It is meant as a friendly cultural acquaintance, not a scholarly study. You will find few statistics here. My focus is on origins and experiences that foster a transcendent sense of cultural belonging. Hopefully, those who question the need for firearms will come away from this read with a better understanding of who gun people are and why they put up such a fight when asked to leave their guns behind.

Gun owners speak their own language, but as you shall read, they have many distinct dialects. They share a rich heritage from which they derive codes of ethics, rituals, and rites of passage that take on all the trappings of a religion. Their core beliefs are even founded in what many would call a sacred document. The US Supreme Court has ruled that gun ownership is indeed an individual right under the Second Amendment of the Bill of Rights, but full-on legal challenges and vicious, media-driven cultural wars continue unabated. This futile turmoil sells millions of guns and tons of ammunition while binding gun culture all the closer. Like infantry, they follow their leaders in relentlessly defending what they see as their very right to exist. Their methods work. You couldn't pick a tougher nut to crack.

Ask me how I know the sensation. I have been a hunter, gun collector, and competitive shooter for well over forty years. Way back there in the 1980s, I even had my own gun shop. Then Wal-Mart came along and drove me out of business. I come from a long line of Virginians and West Virginia mountain people who literally cherish firearms. This is our Appalachian tradition. Seriously, if we had a flag, there'd be a gun on it.

The Hirsh family is not native to the region. My blue-blood great-grandparents made a ton of money—a couple tons actually—and traded their Montclair, New Jersey, mansion for several thousand acres of horse farm deep in the Blue Ridge Mountains. It was an epic cultural collision that might best be described as a *Beverly Hillbillies* in reverse. Much of what you shall read reflects their frequently embarrassing lack of financial restraint. They had a long run at it and stacked up plenty of yachts, cars, airplanes, mansions, horses, and, of course, guns. Our farm has provided us with a haven for all kinds of hunting and recreational shooting. Indeed, it is this fact alone that allowed us to push gun ownership to what some say is the outside edge of the outer limits.

I am a retired high school English teacher and college professor. I specialized in teaching journalism and creative writing. The preponderance of my doctoral level work deals with educational psychology, critical theory and statistics—very useful avenues when looking at cultural paradigms and social evolution. I strive at all times to be objective, and for the record, though I have nothing at all against it, as a researcher, at the time of this writing, I think it important that I not be a member of the National Rifle Association or any other gun lobby group, pro or con. I do appraisals for local gun dealers and broker curio and relic firearms for discerning collectors, but other than that, I have no ties to the shooting sports industry.

As a teacher, school violence in any form shakes me to my core. It is quite a thing to look out at your students and wonder if one of them is packing a gun. I took no comfort in the expulsion of a little girl who wore a charm bracelet revolver to school. I used to tell my fledgling student teachers not to wait for society to prevent an attack, and a smart instructor sets up his or her desk as close to the classroom door as possible so that it can quickly be used as a barricade. When it comes down to the unthinkable, and there is a shooter that cannot be avoided, I stress that, "You, the teacher, are the first one in the way *and* the last one out the door."

Yes, times change, and with the exception of my boys, my extended family's latest generation has all but lost track of the shooting traditions. Some of the overeducated ones swear that they will never understand the gun's importance in a politically correct, postmodern world. I hope to remind them of our family's past, where a gun was just another tool around the house and we took some considerable pride in the fact that every one of us could be trusted to use it safely.

This book does not require the reader to know the slightest thing about the technical aspects of guns. I have dispensed with meaningless reference-book statistics. Instead, I have written five fictional stories that feature guns like characters in sport, self-defense, and military settings. They invite the reader to vicariously pick up the firearm and experience just what it can and cannot do.

"Cold Feet" is my tribute to the shotgun, duck blind, and bird dog. It is an amalgam of personal events set within the greater issue of dwindling natural resources. "The Thirty-Fourth Floor" is a true story recounted to me by a lady hunter/public relations executive who ran afoul of an animal rights activist while stuck in an elevator.

"The Sentinel" is a self-defense story based on a lecture given by the well-known and widely published conservative commentator, David

Horowitz. He argues that gun laws disproportionally disarm those living in poverty. In this case, a single mother has to defend her family.

The two military historical fiction pieces cover a few of the more controversial weapons in our collection. I wish we still owned the antitank gun featured in "The Prototype." "The Fulda Gap" story pits the revered M-1 Garand rifle against the sinister AK-47. These stories serve to represent the veteran's connection to his personal firearm. The weapons' performances are meant to be instructive for those who know little about the actual capabilities of these widely varied guns. With any luck, the narratives will convey the awe that makes owning these sorts of weapons so attractive.

Antigun politicians and media personalities paint a very grim picture of American gun owners. These caricatures are difficult to counter and keep the non-gun-owning public from understanding that there is an entire gun culture at the table, not just an objectionable weapon. My response to this trend is to invite the reader along for the family and friend experiences that weave their way through this text. Let us show you where gun culture comes from. By modern standards, some pretty crazy stuff went down as we wrestled and resisted changing times. There are stories to be told. I had to wait for a few of us to pass on before I could write this book.

The Guns We Left Behind is as much about ladies as it is about gentlemen. Moms, sisters, grandmothers, super models, and lady hunters all have their say. Children, whose formative gun experiences will determine the future of the shooting sports, figure prominently throughout the text.

I don't wish to sound politically correct, but it is impossible to explore gun culture without delving into the twin themes of social class and cultural equity. This book touches on more than who shot what and when. These stories cover eighty years and come complete with all the cliché themes you might expect. My grandparents' generation often merits no sympathy. Rather than disown them, however, I have left in their intolerable world views. Their history becomes the contrast for our family heroes, a whole generation in fact, who forever broke their mindset.

Thank goodness, a few of us continued to farm. Our affinity for the land and love of animals made this book possible. Other Hirshes became doctors, therapists, teachers, accountants, artists, and engineers. We have sent our sons and daughters to fight in World War II, Vietnam, and Desert Storm.

Some of us are religious, but most are not. We seem to be a bland mix of Episcopalian, Catholic, and Jewish faiths. We almost had a Scientologist once, and three of us have seen UFOs. Our politics cover the entire spectrum, from bedrock conservatives to bleeding-heart liberals. Libertarians and independents are on the rise. All life styles are happily represented. We live all over the United States, and we even have a lonely outpost in Israel, where my sister resides with her husband and two sons.

Half of us are good at school and half good at sports. Some of us have trouble staying married. We have both dog and cat lovers, horseback riders, musicians, and card sharks. We produce some of the finest party people in the free world, which I believe is an extension of the Episcopalian in us. Our puritans are currently quite outnumbered, but they're a scrappy bunch. I don't count them out.

In short, we are entirely representative of gun owners today.

My family is a bit eccentric but never *really* criminal. And miracle of miracles, though armed to the teeth, nobody died by gun as we matured with the times. We did have a few close calls, but the multiple layers of safety measures we followed saved us. That being said, we're all half deaf because we never used earplugs in the duck blind. We still hunt and shoot in competitions. Some of us collect a gun or two. If another democrat is elected president, I'm going back into the gun business. But, we don't blow deer off my grandmother's lawn anymore or shoot guns indoors.

*No...heavy sigh...*These days, at least in comparison to my youth, our guns are mostly silent. They sit in vaults and only occasionally make it to the rifle range, woods, and skeet fields. But there is always the potential for a comeback. Maybe we will find a way to satisfy safety and still honor liberty.

Hopefully the pictures that I have added will help to frame the scene.

So, these are our gun culture stories, both good and bad, honestly presented. I hope you find them enlightening

MEADOW LANE FARM

1755 to 2014

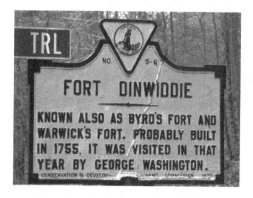

My great-grandfather bought a farm in Bath County, Virginia, in 1920s. Our sixteen hundred acres are surrounded on three sides by the George Washington National Forest. Meadow Lane has allowed four generations of the Hirsh family to hunt and shoot any time the mood takes us. The deer hunting is phenomenal. We are overrun with fox squirrels and rabbits. The groundhog hunting is equally amazing. Shots can reach four hundred fifty yards. Lately, coyotes have become a problem. Thank goodness. I've been waiting.

The farm has always been a place of refuge for our family. As the world grows colder and our futures less certain, a place like Meadow Lane makes the meaning of the Second Amendment stand out. Ironically, my attitude would no doubt mesh perfectly with those who lived on the property centuries before us. As the sign says, Fort Dinwiddie once stood smack dab in the middle of our place. The garrison of Redcoats fought together with local militias against the French and Indians. It seems strange to say it, but at one point in American history, the frontier itself began at musket range, just outside the palisade of this fort. The other side of the mountain belonged to France.

There were all kinds of Indian troubles. People regularly got whacked. My farmhouse stands beside a graveyard where soldiers from the French and Indian, Revolutionary, and Civil Wars are buried.

We know very little about the original Fort Dinwiddie, but according to the historical marker, it did have one prestigious visitor. George Washington inspected this site in September 1755. He returned the following October to consult with Thomas Bullitt who was in command. The garrison was increased to one hundred men after a rather nasty raid in May 1756, but the average number of men was far lower.

Fort Dinwiddie was named after the governor of Virginia who was well aquatinted with the difficulties of maintaining a tranquil relationship with the French and their Shawnee allies. He could muster less than one thousand militia to guard the three-hundred-fifty-mile front. The strategic situation called for a sound military mind, expertise in land navigation, and sufficient charisma to rally the muskets to the king's banner. There were few candidates.

George Washington, though only in his early twenties, somehow sufficiently impressed Governor Dinwiddie to be appointed as a major of militia in 1752. Two years later, he acted as a courier between Dinwiddie and the French. He took a small expedition deep into enemy territory and completed the mission while gathering considerable intelligence about the presumed opposition. The letter he carried back from Fort Boeuf was signed by General Jacques de Saint Pierre who made it quite clear that he was not impressed with the Virginians' defense of the frontier—an observation laden with warlike insinuations.

In March of 1754, Washington was promoted to lieutenant colonel of militia, and he served under General Joshua Fry who was deeply concerned about the tiny garrisons dotted north to south. Colonel Washington took it upon himself to inspect his far-flung, meager forces and made recommendations to better their defenses. Fort Dinwiddie was just another campfire along the cordon and had been under construction for more than two years when he arrived. The pile of miracles needed to build the fort and then to keep it standing has always amazed me.

Fort Dinwiddie was part of an eighteenth-century-frontier, early warning system—the radar of its day. Washington's orders to Captain Hogg in July 1756 were very specific and included a diagram that standardized fort design. He was to proceed southward from Fort Dinwiddie, extending the line. "I have sent you herewith a plan of the kind of forts you are to build, which you must follow exactly." The captain's apartment was to be fifteen feet by fifty feet, and the garrison's barracks was sixty feet by twenty feet. There were designated areas for food storage, and these were to be built over the buried gunpowder magazine. They also were to have a prison cell. Hogg's strategic instructions were simple: "You are to keep out constant covering parties and above all things, guard against surprise."

We do not know exactly where Fort Dinwiddie stood. It was taken down just after the turn of the nineteenth century. We have found a few foundations that match the dimensions of other colonial era chain forts. Based on the geography and the military doctrine of that time, I believe that we may have built a barn over at least part of the original site. Who knew?

As you wander about Meadow Lane, it is difficult not to wonder if you are standing where George Washington stood. The oak sapling that our first president whizzed on is now ten feet around and fifty feet tall. He had to cross the river to reach the fort at the very ford where I fly-fish today. You can't beat it for history.

Colonists were not the only people to leave their mark on the land. There is an Indian burial mound within cannon shot of the fort that date back many centuries. Professors from several universities investigated it when my father was a kid. They didn't find much, as it had been raided many times over the years.

Most of what we know about the period comes from the Warwick family who lived on Meadow Lane more than two centuries ago. Recently, I learned that the original fort was built around their cabin. After the turn of the nineteenth century, the Warwicks and their slaves built what we call the Dinwiddie House, a two story, L-shaped brick home that had fancy mantles around the fireplaces.

This is the only remaining picture of the Dinwiddie House, which was built by Andrew Warwick and his slaves in 1810. Each brick was individually made on site. The house stood literally twenty feet from the original Fort Dinwiddie stockade.

In the mid-1970s, the Dinwiddie House was deemed too dangerous to leave standing. It was gutted for artifacts, and the bricks were salvaged. Each one of them—and there were thousands—was made on the spot by slaves. Perhaps ironically, the slave's cabin still remains and has been restored by my family.

THE SLAVES' CABIN AT MEADOW LANE FARM HAS BEEN FAITHFULLY RESTORED. WRITERS USE IT AS AN INSPIRATIONAL SETTING AND MUSICIANS USE IT AS A RECORDING STUDIO.

The most important and verifiable information comes from the aforementioned Warwick family graveyard. It is obvious that life was indeed short and unspeakably tragic. Children's graves outnumber all of the others. Most of the men buried there are veterans. The region was not considered safe until after the turn of the nineteenth century.

Two hundred fifty years later, though I have traded the horse for a beat-up truck, during hunting season I find myself rolling around the farm with rifle close at hand—just the way every last person who has ever lived here has done. The shooting never totally stopped, though certainly the targets have changed. Thank goodness we settled our differences with the French and related locals. We hardly even chase after the pesky vermin, and they are just asking for it.

But... and this one is a long shot... who is to say what will become of our nation in the decades and centuries to come? Perhaps Fort Dinwiddie will rise again.

WALLAWHATOOLA

Millborrow Springs, VA, 1973

D ear reader, it pains me greatly to report that the private possession of firearms seems to have peaked. Sure, guns will be around for many generations to come, but regulations and taxes will continue to mount. If recent events are any indicator, eventually we will reach a point where only the wealthy can afford the astronomical prices of firearms and ammunition.

That's not the only problem. We are an increasingly urban society. Though the Washington, DC, gun ban was struck down by the supreme court, many cities still forbid gun possession by making ownership a never ending bureaucratic nightmare. We are also running out of places to hunt and shoot. Family farms and gun clubs become freeways and housing developments. Urban sprawl has us in its sights.

At the time of this writing, tens of thousands of gun owners in Connecticut and New York have refused to register their semiautomatic rifles and magazines with the state. Poof! They are all now felons. A Washington, DC, resident was recently arrested for possessing not a gun, or even live ammunition, but simple musket balls and a dud shotgun shell. The ultimate example of how far we have fallen involves a child who was expelled from preschool for nibbling his Pop-Tart into the shape of a gun. Under these conditions, when even ill-intentioned toaster pasties need to be registered, it is easy to understand why gun people are unwilling to work with their opposition.

The long-term situation looks bleak, and worst of all, we're in danger of forgetting when guns were pure fun.

This book is my testimonial about a happier time, when shooters were respected for their skills, and without round the clock television news to highlight the lone gunman's madness, our faith in American traditions was rarely, if ever, shaken. The stories here in span four generations of often joyous hunting, competitive shooting, and collecting. Taken in sum, the narratives reflect a gun culture that we today have all but buried.

THE AUTHOR FIRES A LAHTI L-39 ANTITANK RIFLE. NOTE THE TOP FEED MAGAZINE, SKIS, FOLDING BI-POD, OFFSET SIGHTS AND MUZZLE COVER ON A CHAIN. THIS EXAMPLE HAS BEEN REDUCED TO FIFTY CALIBER AND NO LONGER FUNCTIONS AS A SEMIAUTOMATIC RIFLE.

For me, the ultimate symbol of gun ownership came in its own coffin of a box. As you shall read later on, fifty years ago, my father had a World War II, antitank rifle that, even to this day, could shoot holes right through a Bradley-armored personnel carrier. It was made in Finland and used against the Soviets. The Lahti L-39 was a monster, more than seven feet long, and it weighed well over one hundred pounds. In 2014 dollars it cost him eight hundred bucks. Today's equivalent, a mere 50-caliber pipsqueak in comparison, costs ten grand. All those years ago, military grade rifles and handguns were advertised in the back of sportsman magazines and delivered through the mail. This, by the way, is how Lee Harvey Oswald obtained the Italian Carcano rifle that he might have used to kill President Kennedy.

Now, let's flash forward to our modern-day gun culture. Recently my wife and I joined the only shotgun-shooting club for one hundred miles in any direction. We expected to make some new friends at our orientation meeting. It was a beautiful fall Saturday morning, yet there were no other shooters at the club.

"Most of the time when you come out here, you'll be alone," our guide said. "There are very few truly competitive shooters anymore and fewer still who have the drive to shoot for gold. Ammo costs are way up, and the gas to get here makes it an expensive afternoon." He paused and looked dejected. "The worst part is, there are hardly any kids out here. Where will we find the next generation of skeet shooters?"

I know what he means. I take my boys hunting and target shooting quite regularly, but I don't see many other future shooters in the proverbial pipeline. Those who dislike firearms have etched their antigun shibboleths on our collective societal brain. Aided and abetted by the mass media, educational systems, and even our health care providers, we have come believe the slogan, "Children and guns don't mix." End of story.

Well, they did when I was a kid, and we were the better for it.

First of all, we had toy guns. Lots of them. A great many of these were cap pistols that are very collectable today. We also had toy guns that by modern standards were breathtakingly dangerous. There was no

Nerf. No warning label could cover all the ways that my spring loaded sticker dart gun could send a playmate to the emergency room. I had a Winchester, lever-action toy rifle that launched rather heavy hard plastic .45 caliber bullets. I remember opening it with my dad, but he was the on-duty doctor that night and had to go on a house call before we could try it out. He left me alone with the Winchester.

I was about six, but I understood the pictures on the back of the box that showed a beaming boy and his father *assembling the bullets*. Each cartridge case had a stiff spring in it and a catch for the projectile that held it ready. I loaded the magazine tube. Again, a helpful picture on the box showed me what to do.

I was alone, completely unsupervised. The living room was my shooting gallery, and God help me, our cat, Big Chief Hello, was a tempting target. He'd bitten and scratched me every time I tried to pet him. It was my first experience with guns, animals, and righteous payback. I got off only one, wildly high hip shot before he made tracks. I remember that the lever action actually ejected the empties, and the bullets packed some punch. I shot a hole right through the heavy cardboard box it came in. I was smart enough to shoot at pillows, but eventually I took out a lamp by ricochet. Mom was pissed and took the gun. Dad got an earful too. I got my cold steel back but without the ammo.

My neighborhood pals and I emulated what we saw on TV. The popular shows included *The Rifleman*, *Have Gun Will Travel*, *Combat!*, and *Adam 12*. John Wayne and a young Clint Eastwood still packed the movie theaters. We played a lot of cops and robbers, cowboys and Indians, and war. By the time I turned seven, I had killed my buddies hundreds of times, and they killed me right back. We made our own gun sounds and died as dramatically as possible. We built forts in the yard. Everyone, including parents, knew it was just play. The retired marine corps general who lived next door cheered us on. "Flank 'em, boys! Set up an ambush!"

My summer camp curriculum included learning gun safety and the fundamentals of target shooting in the prone, sitting, and standing "offhand" positions. Just as other sportsmen perfect their tennis swing or putting, we were made acutely aware of breathing, sight picture, and trigger control. Camp Wallawhatoola had a formal rifle range with a fifty foot backstop. We shot heavy, peep sighted .22-caliber, bolt-action rifles at standard NRA, small-bore targets, and we never made a motion unless it was at the range master's command. Our discipline was impressive. Range time was a serious business. The nearby girls' camp taught the same program, which speaks to the universal belief in knowing something about *marksperson* skills. The ladies did have an unsettling habit of giving their rifles cute names.

The owner and director of Camp Wallawatoola, "Uncle Don" Sutton, was a Virginia gentleman who ran a very successful, seven-week, sleep-away program for about one hundred boys. Located deep in the western mountains of Virginia, miles of woods surrounded our camp, and the mighty Cow Pasture River flowed through the middle. I attended from age eleven to thirteen, and I dare say I leaned more about myself at camp than in school.

We called all our counselors *uncle* plus a first name. Some of it was a bit militaristic. We slept as if by squad in large army tents with raised-platform wooden floors. There were dozens of them, and the word *latrine* really did apply when it came to waste management. A bugler played "Taps" every night to officially end the day on a reverent note.

Nobody was going to get sick on Uncle Don's watch. Every five days we went through "weights and swabs," where we all lined up at the showers, towels around the waste, to await inspection. I suppose they wanted to make sure we were eating, so they weighed us. They also looked us over from follicle to toenail for cuts that might become infected. They hit these with liberal coats of iodine. Heaven help the kid with a cut to the face. We came out quite painted.

The five-to-eight boys in each tent were monitored by their resident uncle. At camp meetings Don would shout, "Roll call!" Then the counselors did their headcounts and shouted back in marine-corps style.

"Tent one, sir!"

"Tent two, sir!"

If someone were absent but accounted for in tent five, for example, the counselor would shout, "Tent five—one away and accounted for, sir!"

We were divided into the Blues and the Grays. We fought each other in night-time Capture the Flag, the Naval Battle (in canoes on the river), and something truly insane called the Totem Game, which involved chasing each other through the woods, often in the dead of night. Rivalry was encouraged, but at no time did it ever become unsportsmanlike, and by the way, nobody thought that being a Gray made you a Confederate racist.

Every last one of us was expected to bring a Swiss army knife to camp. We used them for all kinds of things, from whittling to setting up our fishing lures. Our uncles explained the rules about their use. They showed us how to keep from cutting ourselves, as we opened and closed them. Each boy had to step up to Uncle Don for his pocketknife review. He asked questions about rules and how to carve with a knife. When we passed the ten-second test, Don said, "Good man."

I awaited one other annual event with particular interest. Every summer, on the first rained-out day, Uncle Don gave us the "gun lecture."

The uncles spread the wrestling mats out on the pavilion floor, and all the boys took a knee, where they could get in arm's reach, but not touch, Uncle Don's arsenal of perhaps twenty neatly laid-out rifles, shotguns, and pistols. We learned the differences between the guns' actions and calibers. He paid particular attention to each weapon's intended purpose, and he was not afraid to say that self-defense was the number one reason to own a gun. He was pretty graphic about what a .45 could do to a Nazi or home intruder, whichever came first.

Uncle Don painstakingly showed us how to see if each type of weapon was loaded and how to properly handle a gun. Gun safety was his first concern, and he began the lesson with some practical advice. The scenario he described was all too common.

"OK, boys, let's say that you are at your buddy's house with no parents around, and he asks, 'Hey, do you want to see my father's gun?' Don't even wait to say no! You can yell it while you run—not walk—out of the house." Of course we were to tell the first adult we saw about the situation. This is essentially what the NRA's Eddie Eagle gun-safety program teaches kids today. Gun accidents involving children and weapons kept in the home are on the decline nationwide.

I can't remember how Uncle Don got on the topic of hand grenades, but I dimly recall him telling us two things: First, if you come across one, for God's sake, don't touch it. Leave the area *extra* fast. Find an adult. And second, grenades don't actually tick. I suppose you never know what could come back from Germany, Korea, or Vietnam in daddy's duffel bag.

I found the lecture fascinating. Uncle Don always complimented me for asking good questions. I got quite a boost out of that. The gun talk took about two hours and always concluded with a shot from his 1903 Springfield service rifle, the one he carried in World War II.

Apparently Don had endless copies of old catalogs and phone books. He wired them together to produce a fifty-thousand-page-thick target. He was a bit of a showman, as he set this target up against a tree just outside of the meeting hall. This gave us all a good view while shooting safely into the hill. He took twenty giant steps back toward the crowd of would-be marksmen. The *caboom* was the loudest noise most of us had ever heard. I noticed the Springfield's ferocious recoil. Uncle Don willingly put up with serious pain. Admirable. Of course the bullet sailed right through the target and left a rather nasty exit hole. We were all very impressed.

Don spent a good bit of time tutoring us at the camp rifle range. He also gave us a chance to shoot shotguns at clay pigeons. I recall standing up in front of the group to take my two shots at hand-thrown, bright orange birds. None of the boys who went before me, even the super jocks, had even come close to hitting one, and though Uncle Don tried not to show us, he was frustrated with our lack of success.

Looking back, I see that we were too well trained as rifle shooters to make the switch to shotguns. Unlike riflery, where the shooter minimizes movement to the point of squeezing the trigger between heartbeats, with the shotgun, the experts stress that "movement is everything, and everything is moving." If you stop this swinging through motion, you will miss the disk every time. My fellow campers wasted shell after shell.

Then it was my turn. Remember, I was the kid who was always sent to right field in the baseball game because most right-handed batters hit to center and left field. The uncles, however, took great delight in hitting grounders right at me. These always seemed to pop up at the last second to hit me in the face.

Uncle Don barked at me for putting my finger on the trigger before I called, "Pull!" Normally, I was overwhelmed by even the slightest adult snarl. For once, I didn't let it phase me. I just stood up extra straight and did as I was told.

I can still see the birds explode. That sight picture was burned into my brain. When I returned to the huddle, my normally derisive fellow campers were so honestly impressed that they stopped giving me a hard time about my lack of skills in other sports.

I did not mention my country boy advantage. There's nothing quite like growing up on a farm for learning practical shooting skills. We threw down on anything that moved, particularly groundhogs. Conservation was the farthest thing from our minds, because no matter how many woodchucks, squirrels, deer, or rabbits were blasted, the populations consistently rebounded.

That era is now long past, and I miss it. As you shall read, under these conditions the veritable compulsion to shoot guns around the clock, year in and out, caliber by caliber, and gauge to gauge was completely innocent. Our excesses, the cannon, dynamite, and the occasional automatic weapon went largely unnoticed. It was all just another way to stay entertained.

One day, however, I woke up and had to accept the fact that even though I was on my own farm, with nary another human in sight, I was wise not to blast away with my AK-47. Someone would hear the echo and think less of us.

I realized too well that the portrait of the American gun owner had changed. There are no coonskin hats and Kentucky rifles in the new picture. Today, those who know nothing about guns paint over the Lone

Ranger's silver six-shooter and color in the average gun owner's jet-black Glock 9 mm.

I have accumulated several of these politically incorrect weapons. I bought the first one in 1980 as part of my Ronald Reagan survival kit. Every sporting goods store in America sold AR-15s and Ruger Mini-14 rifles. Ammunition was cheap and plentiful. The survivalist mentality became quite fashionable. There were newsstand magazines devoted to the topic.

We were actually worried about a nuclear exchange with the Soviets. Post apocalypse, we figured that biker gangs would come for our beans, so we bought can openers and expensive paramilitary weapons. Nowadays people arm themselves to face down a zombie apocalypse. Just remember, the term *zombie* is code for any threat in your sights.

Assault weapons are photogenic, and not always in a good way. Video that glamorizes these weapons has been characterized as gun porn. AR-15 and AK-47 style rifles scare the hell out of people, and as much as I hate to say it, I think it quite natural that their existence is under constant legal attack. The movement to ban them, however, drives people who might never own a gun right into the gun shop. The neo-gunner looks at the black rifles lining the gun racks and thinks, *Nobody is going to screw with me if I have one of those. And it's only a matter of time before this country is going to implode. Which one to get? I saw one of those on TV. Bruce Willis had one. Or was it Jack Bauer? Nooo, it was Arnold Schwarzenegger, and he had one in each hand when he saved his daughter, Jenny, from dozens of blood thirsty, depraved terrorists.*

The neo-gunner signals the salesman. "Sooo, I'll take two of the black ones please, whichever ones are the most German, and lots of those banana clips. Oh, and loads of whatever bullets go in them. I've got my Visa card ready, and I know I can pass a background check."

In the final tally, antigun rhetoric just makes antigun voter perceptions worse, and the NRA gets the blame. On the other side, gun owners pick up another voter, and gun company stocks out perform gold. Oddly, it is safe to say that antigun politicians like Michael Bloomberg and similarly inclined media personalities drive people to join the NRA and many other pro-gun groups in vastly greater numbers than these powerful institutions can pick up on their own. The NRA's membership actually drops when Republicans are in power.

So why can't we have a societal sit down and work out a solution? The answer to this monumental question is a matter of political policy and so beyond the scope of this book, but consider this: The pro-and-con gun lobbies are actually two halves of a swirling jobs program for thousands of very highly paid people. It begins with a hostile administration giving grants to study gun violence. This money actually subsidizes gun control proponents who conduct studies and wield home spun statistics in a never ending effort to pass antigun legislation and support antigun politicians.

On the other side, the NRA reacts to these attacks and scares the hell out of its membership with, unfortunately, quite plausible political scenarios where one tiny concession turns us into England overnight. Its five million members drag everyone they know to the polls, and together they write one whopper of a community check. I like to remind the harsher partisans that from an employment point of view, solving the gun problem is not in the antigun position's best interest. The hysteria caused by their political overreach actually prevents a meeting of the minds and keeps their lobbyists in profitable and comfortable jobs. I am absolutely certain that the NRA's leaders would actually prefer to let their lawyers go and put their entire focus back on the original missions of promoting the shooting sports and teaching gun safety.

The cycle of outrage and legislation repeats itself whenever gun tragedy strikes. This opportunism galls gun folks, and they deeply resent the underlying inference that all guns are inherently dangerous and their owners potentially deranged. Today, rank and file members of the national gun culture see the relentless litany of antigun activity and sweeping legislation as normal, hypertensive background noise. Only those over fifty can remember a time when there was no red tape or clamor for "common sense" gun laws.

I wonder how Uncle Don would run Camp Wallawhatoola today. Would he even have a rifle range? Could he do the gun lecture without parents signing off on the activity? How many of them would? I can't imagine displaying the modern equivalents of Uncle Don's guns. His were bad ass for their day, but we looked at their wood and steel as an art form. Today, guns are all about science, and function trumps old-world elegance every time.

I can't remember Uncle Don's face, but I do have a picture of him in my mind's eye where he's standing in the rain, aiming his Springfield at the catalog. I wonder where that gun wound up. It would be fitting for it to hang in a veterans' museum, perhaps somewhere in southern Virginia. Again, in my random thoughts, I picture how patrons pass it by without so much as a glance, but I'm there, staring at it.

I know now that it is the 03A3 model with a type-C stock. It is the last American military bolt-action rifle of its kind. I know that Springfields were used in the trenches during World War I. Twenty years later they fought along side the M-1 Garand rifle in the Pacific and all over Europe. Our snipers used them to great effect. The scoped 1903A4's accuracy is still considered legendary. I know that a practiced Springfield armed marksman could crank out a staggering fifteen rounds a minute in a firefight.

Uncle Don's Springfield rifle is a sacred artifact and a powerful talisman. To me, it represents a hundred noble notions that all start with knowing how to properly shoot a rifle.

I don't know how many kids passed through Wallawatoola over the years. I wonder if any alumni lives were saved by Don's safety lecture. Just as importantly, and more to the core of this story, I want to know how many of us joined the gun culture because of summer camp .22s, a gun lecture, and one well aimed .30–06 round. There must still be a few hundred now-grown boys who remain in awe of the 03A3's roar and the slain Sears catalog.

1956: Here we see my father as a teenager showing off a few chucks taken at the farm. Literally thousands of groundhogs have been zapped there over the past seventy years.

Gods of Darkness

Meadow Lane Farm, 1966

My earliest farm memory is of my father and his .220 Swift. I had just turned four. Lyndon Johnson was in the White House. Vietnam seemed perfectly winnable, and people still watched black-and-white TV.

We were rolling around the property in the jeep. Dad was on the prowl for groundhogs. The fields were freshly cut, and a little thunderstorm passed through to put a glisten on the grass. The "whistle pigs" would be out for sure. We were standing atop a hill at a split-rail fence. From this vantage point, we could see the entire valley. Dad pointed out a groundhog, way off in the distance. I looked and looked, but I couldn't see it.

He had the right tool for the job. Every once in a while, a gun gets a name that has no reference to manufacturer or caliber. It's more of a personality thing. The custom-made, Mauser-action heavy barrel .220 Swift in use that day had an engraved name plate on the stock: *Morpheus*. I was told that Morpheus was the mythical god of darkness, but his correct title is the god of dreams and sleep. The symbolism still works.

I recall how my father knelt and leaned into the fence as he laid out the rifle. He flipped off the safety, settled in, and slowed his breathing. I watched him intently as he took his time to set up the shot. Finally, without taking his eye off the target, he whispered, "Hold your ears."

I didn't. I can still hear the crack of that supersonic pill. My ears rang like mad, but I was not scared at all. The shot echoed up and down the valley. We drove down to the bridge, across the river, and way out into the field.

"There he is." Dad picked it up for my inspection. I vividly recall the damage that the fifty-grain soft point had done. It literally tore Mr. Chucky in half. It was my first good look at guts.

"*We* got him." Dad patted me on the head, like I had something to do with it.

It's a curious thing. My father read me bedtime stories. Of course these were mostly about cute little animals learning innocent lessons. He was very enthusiastic about it. He even did their voices. But then, the next morning, we would venture out to catch and kill them. Last night's hippy-hop bunny turned out to be the following day's M-1 carbine bait.

1986: THE AUTHOR WITH HIS CHUCKS. THE WEAPONS CERTAINLY HAVE CHANGED, BUT THE TRADITION REMAINS UNCHANGED. YOU CAN READ ABOUT THIS RIFLE IN THE HUNTING CHAPTER, "'AWG' VERSUS HOG."

That groundhog kill, however, stands out against the fifty-year backdrop of lower species executions. I have a snapshot picture in my mind where I am looking back up the hill to the distant fence from whence *we* shot, and I recall how I truly understood riflery for the first time. The kill was interesting, but it was the shot itself that stuck with me to this day. It remains one of the greatest ever taken at Meadow Lane. I thought, *Someday I'm going to do that.*

Forty-five years later, we used a laser range finder to judge the actual distance, and we now know that Dad made a perfect five-hundred-yard, downhill shot to hit something not much bigger than a carton of milk.

The actual shooting sports run strongly in the Hirsh house. My father was a champion skeet shooter. My cousin is a former Virginia skeet champion, himself. His father was the .410-gauge Virginia champion and a tail gunner who survived World War II. I shot in my first small-bore competitions when I was eleven years old. I have been a mildly successful competitive shooter in two disciplines: high-power rifle and a type of handgun competition known as IDPA (International Defensive Pistol Association).

MY FATHER SUBSCRIBES TO VICE PRESIDENT BIDEN'S STRATEGY AND CHOICE OF WEAPON FOR HOME DEFENSE: THE DOUBLE BARREL SHOTGUN.

My father is a consummate shotgunner, but not always elegant about it. When he really wants to slam something, like an ashtray or an errant household appliance, he'll whip out his ten-gauge, side-by-side shotgun with the minimum legal 18 inch barrels. I must confess that I have only fired that monster a few times. The recoil and muzzle blast are wonderfully and painfully excessive. Dad doesn't seem to notice. In fact, I once watched him use it on the skeet range—that's twenty-five shots inside of ten minutes. He still keeps this gun in the umbrella stand next to the front door with two long, red shells right next to it on the windowsill. Nobody much notices the gun, but every once in a while, someone will say, "Good Lord! What kind of gun shoots those shells?"

Here's a case in point. Years ago, my father was working as a staff psychiatrist at a mental hospital just outside of Baltimore, Maryland. Early on in his tenure, he hosted a cocktail party to entertain his fellow physicians and introduce his family.

I remember a female doctor who asked, "Doctor Hirsh, is that a gun in your umbrella stand? Good God! Are those the bullets?"

Dad drew it out and opened the breech to demonstrate that the weapon was not loaded. Something always seems to come over him when he has that double-barrel ten gauge in his hands. Sixty years of fond memories flow through the gun's old-world wood and steel. He held it proudly and said, "You never know when you're going to have to blow a sociopath off the porch."

As was his intention, everyone laughed. Still, he made a fair point. Those who work with the mentally unbalanced may need to take extra precautions where personal security is concerned. Dad has been at gunpoint several times. Fortunately, he is a consummate therapist who can talk people back from the brink.

Though the sociopath's fate is shrouded in jest, it was this kind of example that became the bedrock of my core beliefs. Comments like that taught me that self-defense with a gun is justified. You don't have to hide it, In fact, it's probably a good idea for people to know what they'll get if they cross that line.

My childhood is replete with these subtle inferences. By the time I reached high school, I was a fully indoctrinated member of our gun culture. My gun safety skills were very finely honed, and I was in the pipeline for full adult participation in the shooting sports. Here lies the take-away lesson of this narrative. When I say that I am objective about the gun issue, understand that I am keeping powerful, formative experiences in check that are the very basis of my character. Going against the gun means a complete reexamination of one's formative years. The gun-control debate will always focus on cold steel, but for the gun owner, something infinitely more essential is at stake.

Yes, when it comes to hunting, on the surface I have become a god of darkness, but to me, as is the case with millions of gun people, firearms are still a source of family lore, love, and light.

Super Models and the Pigeon King

Morgantown, WV, 2011

My son, Forrest, and a few of his fellow college pals came out to the range with me the other day. Our guests had seen video guns, and TV guns, but no 3-D guns. That's what happens when you live in northern New Jersey and Massachusetts. If the Second Amendment is to survive, gun owners need to bring the uninitiated to the rifle ranges and skeet fields. I do it all the time, but this particular trip turned out to be especially memorable. It wasn't just about the guns. It was about my sons.

Forrest and his younger brother, Hunter, have grown up watching me introduce shooting to guests at the farm. My all-time favorite group was a gaggle of New York City fashion models that my stepsister invited. She's an editor at *Cosmopolitan*. (She's a big deal.)

Our farmhouse is isolated and sits above the Jackson River that flows by at the bottom of the hill. When the river is low, all manner of rocks present interesting challenges. The distances are in the fifty-to seventy-five-yard range. I was standing on the porch shooting down the hill into the river. The .22 CB caps fired from my model 9422 Winchester made no real noise. My pellet gun is louder. The girls came out on the deck with their mineral waters and cigarettes (apparently that was dinner), and sure enough, one was game to shoot.

I explained the good points of shooting at the river. "Splash" if you miss. Correct for the next shot, and you will hear a *zing* when you hit. I thought they might shoot once or maybe twice. Instead, they kicked off their high heels and ran through all my ammo before we lost our light. They all wanted another crack at it before heading back to the Big Apple.

The next morning we went to our shale pit and shot my Ruger 10/22. They liked the scope and fired a veritable torrent of bullets at tin cans and clay pigeons lying on the backstop. They were very careful about their nails, and I had to constantly load the thirty-round clips. We even had a stale mega muffin (gas station cuisine) that needed to be bird food.

I can't remember which of them it was, but I heard, "Time to meet your maker, muffin!" Pow-pow-pow. She bounced it all over the range.

"Hey! Don't use up all the bullets! You and your gangsta ways." They cracked themselves up.

As it turned out, these ladies were intensely competitive with each other. They weren't on the runway. They were barefoot in the dirt. They had a long way to go in understanding country life. Their idea of roughing it was walking through Central Park. They thought that stepping on grass instantly kills it and that there were snakes everywhere, perhaps even in the house, which actually has happened twice. One of them had been to a petting zoo and told her friends, "Don't get too close to deer because they bite." Tree frog and cricket sounds worried them terribly. I didn't tell them about all the bats.

Hopefully, once home, they expressed their shock and surprise at the fun they had with an actual gun. They could even say that they had shot a *semiautomatic weapon*. (Gasp!) Their friends say, "Noooo way!" But they think, *Hmmm…was that girl power?*

✛ ✛ ✛

Forrest's gun deprived guests shot .22s of all kinds for about an hour. They peppered paper targets from the shooting bench to learn the basics. We did some plinking from the prone, sitting, and standing positions and even tried a little hip shooting. They learned fast. We reached the main event. They were a little timid with the assault rifles... for about three seconds. They all loved the M-1 carbine, AUG, and AR-180, but what they really wanted to shoot was my Smith & Wesson .357 Magnum. We had tempting water jugs neatly served up at twenty-five yards.

Forrest's friend, Brandon, kept asking, "So can I get one of these back home? Is there anything here that I can get there?"

Learning to shoot handguns requires special attention. I watched Forrest hold the revolver with cylinder open, while his pupil got in position, all sandbagged at the bench. He sounded like a pilot doing his preflight checklist. He handed out the eye and ear protection, and then he said something that I used to say to him every time I handed him one of our pistols, "Focus. Remember—there is nothing more dangerous than a loaded handgun."

Forrest had each friend shoot the .22 revolver first. We destroyed Happy Meal toys. (Always get the toy.) After doing well with the light gun, they moved up to a few .38s fired with the .357. As a capper, he granted their wish and gave each shooter a few full-power 125-grain screamers for use on the milk jugs. They exploded exquisitely. The boys were hooked.

I observed Forrest the instructor. He made no assumptions about the student and watched each one like a hawk. He controlled the bullet supply and who was up next. Best of all, his friends deduced that shooting is something one has to learn. Forrest stressed, "You don't just do this. You need parents who can raise you with it."

Like a good teacher, Forrest was aware of his environment, including the safety habits of those around them. He pointed out good etiquette and marksmanship. He urged his friends to study other shooters and learn the capabilities, makes, and models of various firearms at play.

People who have no experience with guns frequently don't understand recreational shooting and the smile it puts on your face. We were full-on enjoying ourselves. There was a lot of chatting going on between the shooting benches. Friendships were made. Several shooters gave the guys a chance with their guns.

All I had to say was, "These guys are from New Jersey. They've never shot before." It was like throwing red meat to alligators.

"Jesus! First timers? You wanna see why it sucks to live in New Jersey? Try this baby right here. You won't find one of these in *your* gun store."

On the ride home Forrest asked his friends in the backseat, "Did you get enough *wow?*"

They did indeed. Brandon said that he was moving south for sure.

✛ ✛ ✛

Some of Forrest's friends turned out to be good shotgun shooters. Trap and skeet shooting are Hirsh family traditions. My younger son is the best trap shooter I have ever seen. Hunter always does the three-pigeon-at-a-time trick, and he prefers the mini clays because full-size pigeons are "laughably large." He has his mother's perfect eyesight, and most of all, he's quick—real quick.

He was nine years old when he first shot clays. I started him with a .410. It was too small for him, so I let him shoot a twenty gauge. We had one of those cheapo Wal-Mart throwers. The birds flew exactly the same way every time. Hunter is tall, and the full-sized gun's fit was actually OK. He went ten for ten. I had to stop him, but I'll bet he could have kept it up all day. He went from twenty to twelve gauge quickly, and we discovered that success in the shooting sports really doesn't depend on age. Hunter, the twelve-year-old can, beat the grand master—my father.

Hunter doesn't live in his older brother's super-successful shadow. He has his own talents and triumphs. The two of them have one, friendly tussle—on the trap range. Hunter has the occasional lapse in attention where he'll leave the door open for a new champ. But we can't beat him. Hunter is the pigeon king.

✛ ✛ ✛

Forrest called me up the other day and asked for some advice, "As you may know, I'm turning twenty-one in a couple days. What pistol should I buy if I can have just one?"

The first thing I thought was, *Why can you only have one?* Here's my worry, and it is no reflection on Forrest. The economy is not helping discretionary spending. Though current concern about impending gun bans has caused a massive increase in gun sales, fewer guns will be purchased in the future. How is the industry going to survive?

Our computer oriented kids don't buy their guns in the traditional way. My son watches GunBroker.com, and he uses the local gun store as the dealer of record. He pays a flat fee for the instant check and running the gun through the shop's books. Yes, he has to wait a week for delivery, but he saves a ton of money.

Cabela's and Gander Mountain sell a whole pile of guns, and people are only too happy to pay full-sticker price. It's hard for the small storefront dealer to make money with these kinds of competition, yet these small businessmen and women have an expertise that you can't find at the mass merchant whose sales people can only say, "These must be good because people buy a lot of them."

Those few who get a look inside my gun vaults ask me why in the world I would need so many firearms. I explain that I have to think about the future and the guns I will leave behind. Gun ownership is not a sure thing. I have enough that both boys and their kids can rack up one or more of everything they need to hunt, recreate, and defend themselves in a wide variety of scenarios. If the supply of guns were to suddenly be shut off, they will be ready to preserve the tradition, and hopefully, with their votes and grass roots efforts, they will stand up to those who would see firearms removed from our culture.

So…my family's love for the shooting sports has brought us together and made us equals. Range time and hunting have given my boys confidence and good character. We know a trust that those who have no access to this kind of recreation find hard to understand. I know my boys will continue with the mission of spreading the true meaning of gun ownership and all that it entails. Be they wispy super models or boys from the Jersey Shore, people's minds can be changed about guns.

SAINT CROIX

1950

There was a time in the now distant past when the Hirsh family had oceans of money. Our company, Lock Joint Pipe, irrigated the world, including a fledgling country in the Middle East. My grandmother used to boast that her husband brought *the* water to Israel.

My grandfather traversed the earth many times. His first trip around the world took place during what should have been his senior year of college. Yale expelled him for throwing a Coke bottle through an open dormitory window. It hit a proctor in the head. Rather than let the public know of the family's disgrace, the man I knew as "Pop" was bundled off for the Orient and points beyond with instructions to not reappear until his college commencement song hit its final note.

Even without a college degree, my grandfather proved to be a formidable pneumatic engineer. Lock Joint did a lot of work for the military and prospered from the war. He had the funds to go anywhere and do just about anything he wanted. In January 1945, just before World War II was won, Pop rented a seaplane to fly the family to Bermuda.

My father recalls, "I was eight years old and missed Christmas because of a ruptured appendix. That trip was to make up for the lost holiday. There was only one beach open for bathers. The rest were littered with the flotsam and jetsam of a thousand torpedoed ships. American and British troops were everywhere, including the top two floors of our hotel where they installed several naval guns that pointed out to sea. Enjoy the view."

As the twin-engine Grumman sped along, the entire family pressed their noses to the glass to watch for U-boats. "We lived near the Jersey Shore where the Nazis regularly sank freighters and oil tankers. Dinner table talk often wandered to the wolf-pack threat. I remember lying awake at night, clutching my BB gun, as I imagined Nazi monsters sneaking ashore in black rubber boats."

The Bermuda trip was the first of many excursions to the Caribbean islands. In the days before jet airliners made the scene, the flight from New York to San Juan took nine hours. My grandfather boasted that he was among the first to fly above the bad weather in a pressurized-cabin airliner. First-class accommodations and the constant flow of alcohol helped pass the time. The last leg, however, was rather harrowing as they cruised right through storms in a war-surplus DC-3.

Back in those days, only proper people traveled by air, and I am sure that Pop found the experience enjoyably exclusive. Even as a child of the 1960s, I remember how leaving the ground was a coat-and-tie experience. The seats were bigger. The flight attendant was known as a stewardess, and she rocked her own kind of sexy—like Playboy bunnies with wings. I always asked these airborne goddesses technical questions about the aircraft.

"Why don't you come on up to the cockpit, and you can ask the pilots for yourself?" I regularly flew in the flight-deck jump seat.

Looking back, the most glaring difference in air travel was the total lack of security. Nobody's luggage was searched. There were no metal detectors. My great-grandmother bought my father a Beretta pocket pistol in Italy, threw it in her handbag, and got on a plane for home. My teenage father did much the same thing—hence this story.

✛ ✛ ✛

The Hirsh and Lawrence families were fast friends with near limitless cash to throw at their boredom. In 1950 they decided to trade Christmas in frigid New Jersey for three weeks in the Caribbean. They ran into trouble at their connection for the final leg. Apparently the plane was down for critical repair and wouldn't be ready for at least a day.

"Do you have another plane?" my grandfather asked.

"Yes, but it has to be used for another destination."

"I'll buy all the tickets for that flight."

"Sir, that will cost…"

Out came the wads of bills. It was a considerable sum, but Pop and his pal shelled out cash without complaint. Then they invited anyone who needed a ride to just hop on with them. No charge.

It was under these pompous conditions that my father was able to smuggle a double-barrel, .410 shotgun in his luggage all the way from New Jersey to Saint Croix. Broken down, it just fit in his travel trunk. He had eight boxes of shells and doves on his mind.

This was the third trip to Saint Croix in as many years. When in the islands, most tourists look out to sea. Not Dad. He knew the island's interior and its primitive roads rather well. It was on one of these expeditions that he made a major discovery; there was a gorge where thick flocks of fat doves swirled endlessly. It was a hunting prospect yet unequaled in his experience, and he vowed that the next trip to Saint Croix would be very different.

✦ ✦ ✦

The rental car driver stomped on the accelerator as the gunner leaned out the passenger side window. Their efforts to hunt doves on foot had been disappointing, but they were critical thinkers. The birds they were after had an annoying tendency to scatter from the road just outside of .410 range. The solution was to use the car to accelerate and overtake the fowl before they could escape the pattern of seven-and-a-half-sized shot. This required a serious head of steam. But there were few cars on the island, and the hunting ground was remote. In fact, the boys had never seen a car on the flat dirt road.

Philip Jr. and Kyle were fourteen and thirteen years old respectively. They spent a great deal of time on their farms shooting every kind of gun imaginable at frequently inappropriate targets, but nobody seemed to mind, or even notice, their breathtaking antics. In this case, nobody minded that they were driving one of the rental cars. The adults had no idea where the boys were, and they really didn't care. If they could have heard the gunfire, they might have looked up, but the chances were good that no matter what the boys did, it would be dismissed.

Dad says that, "My father was just weird like that. He could tear your head off for lighting a match, but you burn down the barn, and he didn't say a thing. We'd been shooting guns and driving vehicles on our own for years. Don't forget that I had a BB-gun room in the attic at the house in Montclair, New Jersey, and a rifle range in the basement."

Today we would describe this dove-hunting style as a drive-by shooting. Their system, however unsporting, worked well. They returned to the resort and dropped the birds at the back door to the kitchen. They were plucked and served with a special sauce. Again, not a single adult wondered why dove was served on a Caribbean island. Night after night the birds became an expected staple.

Three weeks dwindled down to the last day of the trip. The boys had two shells left. They revved the car and streaked down their well-traveled runway. Just as Kyle was about to fire, a car came around the bend. He panicked and attempted to get the gun back in the vehicle. In so doing he hit the hammers on the dashboard, setting off both barrels.

The shot blazed "harmlessly" between his arm and abdomen and passed through the seat and hit the beam between the front and back doors with enough force to swell the frame and keep it from properly closing thereafter. The final ricochet shredded the back seat.

The boys were obviously mortified, but quite intelligently they decided to play a low card. They parked the car in front of the hotel, as usual, and walked away. The next morning a wondrous thing happened. The men hopped in the undamaged vehicle, and the ladies took the battered wagon. The shrapnel wounds did not fit anything in their feminine frame of experience. To them, the car's sad state was almost quaint, an obvious symptom of the third world that they had graced with their money and inexhaustible pomp.

They parked the cars at the airport, hopped on their chartered plane, and returned to San Juan, where they partied it up for a few more days. My father waited for the ax to fall, but as usual, he got away with it.

HOME ON THE RANGE

Montclair, NJ, 1985

Dad loves to tell stories about his misspent youth. Many of these involve guns fired indoors. Knowing him, the content was quite believable but a little hard to picture.

A few years back, while on a drive to New York City, Dad announced that we were taking a detour to visit his childhood home in Montclair. Just as I was told, the neighborhood was opulent in the extreme. Massive mansions lined the streets. Luxury cars filled the driveways. Gardeners toiled around the boxwoods and gazebos. I was a little apprehensive about knocking on the door to ask for the grand tour. Sure enough, the owners knew about the famous, eccentric Hirsh family, and they were only too happy to show us around the house.

We went down to the spacious basement. Dad led us to the farthest corner of the room. He opened a four-foot square, plywood panel that was waist high off the floor to access a chamber behind a fireplace in the servants' quarters.

He called me closer to look inside. "You see that metal plate? You can open it to clean out the ashes from behind the fireplace in the other room. Saves a lot of mess."

The homeowner asked, "Interesting that you start here. I have wondered how those little holes in the panel got there."

"Bullets." Our guide was aghast. Dad reached in and lifted the access door from its hinges and dragged it into the light. "Here we see two things. Notice this rough area. That's from the zillion .22s I shot down here when nobody was around. Some of the deeper ones were from a Nambu Jap pistol I got from Uncle Gene. I leaned this plate at an angle, and the bullets mostly went straight down into the dirt. I made the ricochet work for me. Then one day, I decided to try it with my father's Springfield .30-06."

"Oh my God!" The owner wasn't smiling.

I added, "Sounds reasonable. I'm sure you were scientific about it."

"My dear boy, I am a doctor and scientific by nature. My every move is devoted to the scientific method. Notice how I use my powers of observation."

He called our host to look a little closer at the metal target.

"Here, we see *the* hole, just as I shot it some fifty years ago. It's .30 caliber, or 7.62 mm if you'd like to go with the metric system."

"I prefer the metric. In light of this evidence I can only conclude one thing. This, of course, proves that with remarkably little preparation a .30-06 can indeed be shot indoors."

"I agree with you. Let's go around the corner and take a close look at the fireplace." He dropped the hatch back into place.

The owner looked quite pale while we inspected the hearth. We laughed about it, but our host shook his head. "This was insanity. Where did the bullet wind up?"

My father used a fireplace poker to show the trajectory. "Well, it went right along this line, about aorta level I should think, right through a couch, but it was just a tiny hole and ended up here." He pointed to a spot on the opposite wall. "See? I filled in the hole with Ivory soap, and it blended perfectly."

We left the depths of the house and ventured up to the attic to see the BB-gun range. The shooting gallery was well lit by sun and electric lights. One could take a rather long shot, but there was one small flaw. The backstop was a series of glass window panes.

"Occasionally I misjudged things and took out some glass. There was a pile of replacement panes in the garage. I was eleven years old, but I figured out how to repair a window. Finally, I ran out glass. Once again, nobody noticed, or for that matter, would have cared."

THE LOST IDEALS OF NAKED MEN

Warm Springs, VA, 1953

The Warm Springs Pool is a popular destination in Bath County, Virginia. The prolific mineral water spring spouts its medicinal luxury at a perpetual 98.6 degrees. The structure that covers the forty-thousand-gallon pool has remained unchanged since it was first opened in 1761, which, by the way, makes it the oldest spa structure in North America.

George Washington visited the pools long before anyone even thought of building on the site. He first hopped in while on an inspection tour of nearby Fort Dinwiddie. One wonders if his creativity instigated construction.

The designers had a unique problem. They knew that they could not cover the moist heat and steam rising from the pool. Their solution was to build a dome that covered the walkways and changing rooms but left the pool itself open to sun and moon. The uncovered rafters meet at a massive post that rises twenty feet, dead center of the pool.

Except for the deep winter, people take the waters in all kinds of weather. On cold, late-fall days, steam rises around the bather like a plume. That's pretty cool, but taking the plunge during a rain shower is my personal favorite. I like to watch the storm from beneath the surface.

The men's pool has a circumference of 120 feet and is six to seven feet deep. The lady's pool is much smaller and shallower. Depth is maintained by increasing or decreasing the flow of spring water over the spillway. The boards that act as baffles can be set from trickle to tidal wave. People actually pay extra to go below and sit up against the dam with their backs to the torrent. The attendant then opens the boards to let hundreds of gallons of pounding "water treatment" massage the patron's pains away. Just don't let go of the safety rope, or you will be swept under the wall and out into Warm Springs Run.

Somewhere along the line, a cold pool was added on the men's side. You could cannonball from one to the other in about five steps. Temperature wise, it was like going from the womb to the Arctic Circle. The shock to the system was not for the faint of heart. Eventually they had to fish a stiff out of the ice bath, and so the cold pool is no more.

The Warm Springs Pool offers some rather unique physical challenges. The acid test is to swim the circumference of the pool underwater. I had to grow into it, but by the time I hit my early teens, I could stay down longer and go father than my old man.

This competition was not without its dangers. The swimmer must shoot under the bleacher style steps either at the start or the finish of his run. It is a tight fit and a scary twenty-five feet. It is by far easier to flip over on your back and then, going hand over hand, pull through to the big rock on the far side of the tunnel. From there, it is best to push off and glide as far as possible along the wall, which, according to the ancient rules, must never be more than an arm's length from the swimmer.

Another activity that required underwater endurance involved hovering on the bottom in search of ancient treasure. We had no diving masks or weight belts to help us. The underwater world was completely out of focus. We sifted through the rocks and sand, one handful and lung full at a time. Visitors often saw the pool as a wishing well and tossed a coin in as they left. Over the years we found the grist of their wishes, which included buffalo nickels and Indian head pennies.

Times change. Nowadays such aquatic athleticism is frowned upon, and digging for coins is positively forbidden. These changes were to be expected, and we never really concerned ourselves with the posted rules anyway. We should have seen the ultimate change coming.

Women are now allowed in the men's pool.

That one came as a shock. I didn't realize that this tidal shift had occurred until a few months ago. I had been away from Warm Springs for a while. I came back for deer season and took my buck just after first light. We cleaned it and had it hanging by nine a.m.

"Let's go to the Warm Springs Pool," Dad suggested. "It's open for a few more days. Last chance till next Easter Sunday."

Never was there a more well-intended idea. I was all smiles as I walked in. I looked at the sky reflected on the water. That's when I first saw a very feminine, leopard-print bikini bottom broach the surface. It was aimed right at me. For a split second I thought, *That can't be a guy's…Oh my God…there are women in the water.*

We walked over to the new, separate Jefferson Pools office to find out what the hell happened and when. We found a gift shop and a masseur who wanted a king's ransom to be admitted to the pool.

I looked at my father. We were both speechless.

We stumbled back to the car. "Dude," I said, "we're drowning in political correctness. It's like there's no point in going anymore."

People still come to take the waters for their intended, healthful purpose. Cars pile up in the driveway. Quite rightly, patrons feel privileged to bask in the same setting as some pretty famous guys.

In President Jefferson's day, the pool was said to cure all manner of ills. Proper decorum was followed, and bathers wore robes. They strongly believed that one could indeed have too much of a good thing. Nobody ever, and I mean *ever*, spent more than ten minutes in the watery fold.

Jefferson visited the pools on various occasions between 1818 and 1825. Always the Renaissance man, this scientific American hypothesized that the length of time one spent in the pool was immaterial. If fact, his observations over many years showed that a good, long soak was endlessly beneficial. However, he once spent a shocking, death defying forty-five minutes in the pool and promptly came down with a dangerous influenza that, obviously, he survived. He had to admit that his hypothesis about the benign effect of the waters was still in dispute.

Other presidents who have visited the pool include McKinley, Taft, Wilson, Coolidge, Hoover, Franklin Roosevelt, Eisenhower, Lyndon Johnson, and Nixon. The list of famous ladies includes Jackie O, Margaret Truman, Mamie Eisenhower, and the Duchess of Windsor.

Robert E. Lee wrote his final letter to his wife from the Warm Springs Pool. John dos Passos, James Thurber, Douglas Fairbanks, and Arthur Murray all took a soak. The list goes on and on.

We Hirshes might not be famous, but my father believes that our family should win the most frequent visitors of all-time award. He told me, "My only swimming lesson was in 1941 when Father tossed me off the steps in front of the attendant's room. I remember it being a desperate and mercifully short distance back to the steps, but I went from wimp to Weissmuller in ten seconds."

The lessons learned involved far more than how to stay afloat in water. First, this was an old-world men's experience. Unlike the ladies in their pool, male bathers were nearly always nude. We thought nothing of it. There were zero sexual connotations. But now there is a new modesty afoot, and it's bathing suits for all. I suppose it hasn't harmed the experience. Too few of us remember how things used to be to mount any sort of defense against these changes, and even if we did, how would the public perceive our objections? As sexist? Or perhaps elitist?

Perish the thought.

The Warm Springs Pool also taught me a great deal about race relations. Bath County Virginia in 1969 was not known for a progressive attitude toward people of color. The only African Americans I knew worked for my family or the Homestead Resort, which owned the pool at Warm Springs. My grandfather was prone to racism and bigotry, but my father did not share this attitude at all. This difference was on display every time we went to the pool.

We had an almost familial relationship with the "colored" gentleman who took the money and gave you towels. Dad remembers Horace who ran the pools in the thirties and forties. The elite had mint-julep parties complete with an armada of little silver boats in which to float their drinks. Horace watched several generations of Hirsh men paddle through. I learned a great deal from watching Dad, Horace, and his successor, Steve, interact.

First, both men enthusiastically shook hands, smiled and made eye contact with each other. Dad told me recently that, "They were gentle, forbearing men who had a lot more class than many of the men in the water."

It was always the same greeting. "Well, Doc! How ya doing?"

"I couldn't be better. How's the family?" This wasn't an empty question. They talked quite a bit. Sometimes Dad gave medical advice. They told each other jokes and made vague references to past antics at the pool.

Steve lived on tips. He would towel off your back for an extra dime. We toweled off our own posteriors, but Dad always gave his friend ten dollars as we headed out the door. At the time, this was not an inconsiderable sum. I understood that race played a part in who had all the power. But I also saw that this wasn't natural and good people did what they could to help those so unjustly trapped by a southern social scene that had not budged appreciably since the Civil War.

They also shared a secret. Both men knew that the best time to play at the Warm Springs Pool was either in the middle of the night or in the dead of winter. Horace knew that the boys were slipping in, but he covered for them.

At first the windows were nailed shut, but the spillway chute that feeds into the local stream was large enough for a brave swimmer to duck under the wall and pull himself against the considerable wash through to the pool. My father and his fellow dove-hunting friend, Kyle, liked to visit when the pool was at its most spooky.

At first they pulled innocent pranks, like throwing all the doorknobs in the pool or perfectly arranging all the cheap pine chairs on the bottom. It took a few years, but eventually the boys realized that they could use the pool for a scientific study of how bullets behaved when shot into water.

When not actually fishing in the Jackson River that passes through Meadow Lane, my father and his friends shot at fish that strayed too close to the river bank. This is actually far more difficult than one might think. The target's depth is critical. Its image is also refracted by the water, and aiming right at it will cause a miss every time.

Their experiments involved two variables. The first was a study of penetration by caliber and bullet type. The second was a study of how to aim at underwater targets. They were quite methodical about it, which is testimony to their prep-school educations. They faced considerable cold when not in the water, but they were both very determined, rugged kids who routinely shook off bad conditions in a quest for cutting-edge fun. How they did not catch Jefferson's influenza is beyond me.

Their lab was quite simple—the original myth busters weighed down a changing-room chair with stones from the bottom of the pool. It sat five feet below the surface. They took turns sitting in it to observe bullets fired point blank into the water. Of course they watched from the side to see how far down the projectile could go. Then, from an extra generous distance, they watched the bullets and shotgun blasts as they came straight on.

My father remembers, "For the record, the shooting was done in daylight, in the winter when the place was solid shut and available 24-7, if you knew how and had the balls to do it. In the winter one other challenge was to shimmy up the center pole—ice and all, don't get splinters in your sack—then hand over hand out on a rafter and drop in. We never had even a close call. No cop ever came by, no matter what the racket. In those days, before the ski slopes opened, everything in the area was closed, except the Homestead itself."

A few of their experimental artifacts remain. "We used to have a wooden toolbox in which the muzzle loading stuff was kept. If you have it, take a look in the tray. Among the brushes and screws, you may find a spent .32 bullet (possibly .380, if memory isn't serving) as I used to keep it there. It was one of the slugs I 'caught' underwater in the pool. Kyle and I each kept one, and while it sounds silly today, at the time we made a deal: if either of us was in a bad spot and needed the other to come immediately, sending the bullet would be the signal. Just why the phone wouldn't have been more expeditious doesn't factor into this sort of fanciful bonding arrangement."

No matter how corrupted its status, the Warm Springs Pool represents family, natural wonder, and history. Once you are in the water, it's 1761 all over again. More profoundly, for me, the pool became my church. Watching a rain storm from within the pool was the homily. Swimming the circumference was a pilgrimage. The waters offered me unction, a periodic cosmic oiling that helped me stay focused as I sailed along.

I shall not forget the last time my father and I were in the pool. It had been a while, and I wanted to test myself in the traditional ways, but I couldn't hope to try the underwater challenge. There were too many motionless bodies in the way. They hung onto those silly, hot-pink foam noodles. Sometimes they rode them. I'll leave that image to you. A sign said, "Any objects found in the pool are the property of the owners."

"The cold pool would thin these guys out real quick," I said.

"Yeah. This looks bad for us." We were quiet for a while. We waited for the crowd to pass, but just as soon as one lawyer or dentist got out of the water, he was replaced by a banker or worse.

By Jefferson's standard, we should have died. We pulled out of the driveway and headed back to the farm. "Just think," Dad rambled, "of how many famous men have pissed in the pool. Some of those types of guys travel with an entourage. You know the kind I mean. They are always suck-ups and sycophants who all secretly hate the bastard they work for and probably for good reason. I'll bet the minute their anointed one went down below the dam for the water treatment, all his boys bobbed their way over to the spillway, and while hovering, amid the casual chat, they let their waters intermingle in his wash."

"What a luxury."

"Yeah. There are few equals. Take it from a guy who has been in the water for seventy years, the Warm Springs Pool affects everyone differently."

"You ought to know."

"Damn right. A good long soak makes philosophical people pose their thoughts. It soothes the hypochondriac and inspires the historian. I have noticed that it makes you a little spiritual, which normally would worry me, but even I, the greatest of atheists, have to give you a pass when we are in there. As for me, I don't regret pumping a few hundred rounds into the pool. In fact, it elevates us to a pretty special status."

"Us?"

"Well, Thomas Jefferson, Kyle, and I have something in common. We are the only scientists to conduct experiments in the Warm Springs Pool."

STAR STUDENT

Meadow Lane Farm, 1972

The first time I ever fired a handgun is really two stories that start off differently but end in the same place. First, I must tell a horror story.

My father's relationship with his father was always a bit *strained*. It all started with despicable parenting. For instance, the traditional toss-the-toddler-up-and-catch-him game is supposed to build trust between parent and child. My father's experience was just a little different. Most of the time, the play was normal, but every once in a while, quite at random, Pop would deliberately *almost* drop him. "He would catch me at the last possible second, about a millimeter off the ground, and instead of saying 'upse daisy!' I heard 'nigger baby!' I learned early on to simply stay the hell away from Father if at all possible and take my revenge where I could find it."

Philip Reid Hirsh Senior, my grandfather, was a very difficult man. But, he was not without some significant positive traits. First among these was his willingness to spring for our private educations at some of the finest prep schools and colleges in the country.

Pop valued knowledge and critical thinking skills, particularly as they related to architecture and engineering. Report cards were a very big deal. One had to stand before the veritable bar and pass review. Even thank-you notes were graded for grammar and spelling. I had to fight my way through problems with attention deficit disorder, undiagnosed dyslexia and serious emotional issues, but by the time I reached high school I regularly earned excellent grades in English, history, art, drama, music and foreign languages. So, naturally, Pop focused only on my grades in math and chemistry. The insinuation was that my poor performance was due to a lack of character. He had no idea that his thoughtful guidance made every math test feel like a life or death experience.

I also have to give Pop some points for having survived his own hellish childhood. His subsequent parenting, even at its worst, was an improvement on what he endured during his tender years. Though he was emotionally repressed, I think my grandfather was capable of introspection and even feelings of guilt, but he never learned how to reconcile internal conflicts, only burry them or buy off the offended parties.

Somewhere between Yale and the yacht club, however, Pop did come up with a few humanizing quirks. For example, he loved costume parties which he often attended in drag. Apparently he was really into it. I say more power to him. I would have been very supportive.

As the many trophies in the family display case attest, Pop was a life long athlete who played both golf and tennis quite respectably. As a young man he lettered in track and baseball. He was a fearless and ambitious outdoorsman with rod and camera. In his later years, Pop toned things down to sports that were equal parts ball and sipping scotch. He was good at bocce ball, but absolutely deadly at croquet.

Pop's social circle took their mallets and wickets rather seriously. They came from all over to test him on Meadow Lane's perfectly groomed and leveled croquet course. Here's the endearing part. Pop's brave challengers thought that they were playing on an official set up, but Pop actually scaled it down ever so slightly to match the length of his average hit. This threw the competition just enough to give him an advantage.

Pop was mercurial with family. A one-on-one meeting with him was a terrifying scenario. This was the guy who often said that one of the best parts of running a business is getting a chance to fire people. I do believe he would have fired me if he could. He knew just how to reel me in. One second he was all compliments and jokes, but the very instant he saw me relax, bam! He'd go all prosecutor. Every mistake ever made could come back up for review. It was always better to see him when there were guests around because he loved to show off even more than stunting my emotional growth.

Cocktail parties were particularly challenging for those poor, unfortunate Hirshes that were sucked into the scene. We tend to be a family of collectors, and my grandfather had exquisite knickknacks from all over the world. Guests loved to hear the stories behind each piece. "Oh that…" he'd say. "I picked that up in Nairobi. I had to dodge three lions and a rhino to get it. It's an interesting story. You'll see it all in the slide show."

Pop was well read, relatively witty, and quick with a pun. Most of all, he was a consummate chef. His restaurant, the Gristmill, was a five-star experience in a cute, but otherwise two horse town. Those who brushed up against Pop's act thought him unique, and they coveted his attention.

It was early fall in Virginia. My parents had recently broken up because my mother committed what we have come to call an indiscretion with one of the Austrian ski instructors at the Homestead Resort. The divorce was swift. Pop was exuberant with the news that my mother was out.

We were sitting at the breakfast table. Pop had made his awesome pancakes, and the freshly drawn maple syrup bade me eat about fifty of the things. Out of nowhere, Pop launched in on what a mess my mother was and how he had always thought her spoiled and a lush.

My father recounts that moment. "God damn! The irony of his saying that, even as mad as I was with your mother, was almost more than I could take. He was talking like this right in front of you. I was furious, but there was no point in saying anything. You remember how we got even?"

I do. It was one of the great immature moments that periodically popped up in my childhood. I wasn't making the mistake. That was done for me. I was an apprentice/accomplice.

Now, at this point, another story intervenes.

Pop had Meadow Lane's farm manager plant an annual garden that gave us fresh vegetables for almost half of the year. My grandfather took great pride in what "he" had grown. Just like everything else in his twisted values system, legumes offered the opportunity for bragging rights amid a select society.

The average annual income in Bath County, Virginia, in 1972 was about a dollar and a half. Poverty was rampant. Land was dirt cheap, and the wealthy gobbled up vast tracts. These jaded few had lavish farms with air strips and horse barns. Competition among the ruling class was fierce. It was mostly wallet warfare, as in who had a new Rolls Royce, Cessna aircraft, swimming pool, or guesthouse. They played endless games of golf, croquet, and tennis at the Homestead Resort whose opulence offered them a social oasis. They could ballroom dance, fine dine with minority service, hit the spa for a massage, shoot skeet, or have a horseback ride all in the same day. They were served tea at four o'clock in the massive, two-story football field of a lobby. They sipped to sonorous harp and piano melodies played by ladies in flowing gowns.

Seriously, the whole scene warped my world view. Noblesse oblige still exists, and I had to earn my place in the landed gentry. There were complex social customs and traditional skills to be learned. Some were fun, such as ski lessons. But like my father, I had to attend the resort dance school, and my table manners were finely honed. Chilled forks and finger bowls didn't surprise me.

The well-to-do sought to out pomp each other's dinner parties and weddings. They would do just about anything to win the spotlight. You name the event, and I could show you near universal intrigue, spying, and even social espionage.

The pinnacle event at the end of summer was the county fair and the vegetable judging competition. Pop was a pumpkin man, and 1972 was to be an orange-banner year. His garden's blessed mound of hyper fertilized, probably radioactive soil, produced a pumpkin a full three-feet tall and four-feet wide. It weighed about seventy-five pounds.

It is here that the stories run together again.

The breakfast table ex-wife bashing left my father in a foul mood. We escaped Pop's clutches and were back in our farm house across the way. I was thinking of going fishing when my dad came out on the porch. He had his Star model B 9 mm pistol in his waistband.

"Hey, son, we have a secret mission to complete."

I was happy to be included, but I was a bit confused when we backed the jeep up to the vegetable garden. It took some doing, but we loaded up the world-beating pumpkin and took it down to a shallow part of our river. We backed up to the bank and dropped it in the water. It sat stationary on the bottom, but a good two feet rose above the stream.

Dad handed me the pistol. He told me how dangerous it was and stood right behind with his hands outstretched, ready to take over should I screw up.

"Hold on tight as I rack the slide. There. It's ready to go. The safety is off. Shoot the pumpkin." I leveled the sights, and using a Weaver stance, squeezed the grip for all it was worth. I had to make a twenty-five-yard shot. Much to my surprise, the recoil was manageable, and I hit the target.

Bang! "Good shot. Shoot again." Bang! "Good, a little high. Watch your trigger pull. Just like the rifles." Bang! "Good! Unload on it!" Bang! Bang! Bang! The slide locked back.

I hit the pumpkin several times, but the full metal jacket bullets didn't have much effect. Dad expected this and trotted to the jeep. He came back with some dynamite fuse and a whopper can of black powder. He waded out and cut a hole in the pumpkin top, ripped at the innards, and shoved his bomb inside. He lit the fuse and yelled, "Run back behind the jeep!"

Up to this point I had never seen a homemade explosion. (There would be many to come.) I had missed the era of hand grenades in the trout pond and dynamited beaver dams. I did, however, once see a clip of 8 mm movie film shot by Dad and Kyle that involved a pick-up truck's death by dynamite. It was part of a movie-making project they called *The Epic*.

The pumpkin explosion mushroom cloud blew chunks well over a hundred yards. Some of these pelted the jeep. One piece came straight at me, and I dodged it at the last possible instant. The rest fell into the river to take the current.

Dad produced another clip for the pistol. "Let's shoot some moving targets."

The pumpkin's remnants were excellent fodder, but shooting from the bank down into the river at a steep angle threw me. Dad showed me the proper sight picture, and I managed to hit my share. After the operation, as I field stripped and cleaned the Star B, I felt a certain amount of pride in my pistol craft, which gave me a much-needed boost in self-esteem. I couldn't throw or catch a baseball, but I could handle a semiauto pistol. Back in those days, marksmanship was a desirable skill.

As for Pop, he was baffled by the great pumpkin's disappearance, but he knew plenty of people who would do anything to keep him from winning first prize. He never stopped looking for the culprit, but his investigations took him in the wrong direction. To this day, his frustration makes me smile.

THE SENTINEL

The Projects, Modern Day

Debbie Thomas was a light sleeper. She had to be. For most people, things that go bump in the night are imaginary. We wake up, shudder, and shake it off. That being said, there are places on this green acre where that bump means business. Debbie lived in Bump Central Station, a low-income apartment complex surrounded by the remains of industries that had long since gone to China. For the kids in the burbs, it was all bedtime stories and "'night,' night; sleep tight." For

Debbie's three small children, the expression "pleasant dreams" was an absurd proposition. They joined hands, and on their knees they prayed for protection before they turned out the lights.

The police and emergency medical teams were equally unlikely to venture into the Projects without a veritable squad of marines to give them cover. Between the overdoses, domestic disputes, stabbings, and shootings, there was plenty of business for both agencies. But neither service would show before the shooter had fled, and the only medical attention needed was a body bag.

Debbie knew that if she had a problem with the locals, she was on her own. With no husband and two low-paying jobs, she was just barely keeping their heads above water. She had fifty dollars saved to buy one essential appliance—a handgun.

She bought a well-used Jennings .25 automatic and ten bullets from a pawn shop whose manager was sympathetic to her problem. Like so many people living in poverty, Debbie had no driver's license. Normally, legally, this would be a problem when buying a gun, but the little .25 was off the books. She had no place to shoot it, though the proprietor showed her how to load and unload it. She practiced the motions as he explained everything that could go wrong.

Debbie was painfully aware of how the lesson ended. "It isn't much of a gun, but it's better than nothing."

The armed, single mother waited for the subway in a tightly packed crowd of commuters. She reached into her coat pocket and palmed the little pistol. *I wonder if anybody else has an illegal gun in his pocket.*

June was a bad month in the complex. The warm weather drew tenants outside, and territorial confrontations were predictably on the rise. Gunshots were common. Debbie and her children worked out an emergency plan. The kids went to their room, pushed the dresser in front of the door, pulled the mattress off a bed, and hid under it in the closet. She stayed outside to do what she could. She did not say what that would be.

Weeks went by, and Debbie had the gun ready several times. But mercifully, the danger passed them by. Her children grew proficient in their drill. Ultimately, there was a gun battle on her floor. One of the combatants was caught in the open of the corridor, and rather than take a bullet, he hit the nearest door. It was double locked, but it gave way instantly.

Debbie hid behind the kitchen counter, terrified beyond belief. Her heart pounded with adrenaline, but her instinct to protect her children allowed her to focus, even with tears streaming from her eyes.

Load the gun. Check to make sure it is ready. Sometimes they jam before they are even fired. Hold it firmly. Push the safety catch to red. Look at the target. Point the pistol at the middle of the attacker's chest, and fire as many times as possible. Above all, if you are going to shoot, shoot first.

She did. The pistol jammed on the third shot, but rounds one and two connected. The assailant's eyes went wide in disbelief as he succumbed to his wounds. She stood her ground but gasped for air. Her fear gave way to anger.

"That's what you get!" she growled. "You don't come into my house!" She heard her children call for her. "Stay in your room! Tisha, keep your brothers in there."

The smell of gun powder lingered. A low voice came from the hallway. "Hey in there, mama, don't shoot!"

"I have children in here! Stay the fuck out!"

"I know it. If you don't want to be killed by that dead man's friends, you'll let me get that fuck out here in the hallway. I'm putting down my gun. I'll show you both hands. I'm coming in. Take it easy now. Nobody is going to hurt your babies. I got some of my own. I'm trying to help you."

"Why? You come in here, and you're a dead!"

A hand reached out and slowly lowered a silver revolver to the floor in her doorway. "We are going to start helping each other."

Debbie held her fire, but she was shaking so badly that she couldn't have hit the doorway, let alone someone coming through it.

"I'll kill you if you make me!" Debbie kept her tiny weapon trained toward the danger zone.

True to his word, the unknown gunman dragged his dead enemy out into the hallway. Two other men then threw the body down a stairwell. The .25 automatic-bullet wounds hardly bled, and aside from the broken door, there was no evidence leading to her apartment.

"I'm coming back in. There's something you need to see." Open hands showed in the doorway, and for the first time Debbie saw a man, not just a threat. He was near her age, a little gray, with tired eyes.

"Your gun is jammed. You see the empty bullet stuck in there? Find the empty cases and get rid of them and that gun," he said. "Don't feel bad. This fucker had it coming. You picked a good one to shoot. You did the right thing. You understand? You had to do it. Hell, you might have saved my life, not to mention your neighbors'."

Debbie offered him her pistol, and he took it. In a soft voice, he said, "Don't tell anyone what happened here. Ever. Make sure the kids know to keep quiet. None of your neighbors are going to say shit or ask any questions. You understand? This never happened."

She nodded. He cleared the jam and removed the clip. "How did you keep this away from the kids? They know you shot somebody. They'll always be curious about guns. That's when there's trouble, you understand?"

"You take it. I don't know if I could do that twice."

"You got lucky tonight—this little piece of shit against a man with a 9 mm in one hand and a .45 in the other. Really, it's a miracle you're sitting here."

Debbie's eyes welled. "Yup," she choked, "musta been our prayers."

"Go to your kids. You have a lot to get straight. Let us take care of the rest."

Debbie felt sick as she huddled with her weeping and terrified children.

"We're safe. It's all right. Mama's here. I'll protect you. You go ahead and cry. I'm here. I'm here for you. I love you. It's going to be good." She rocked her babies in her arms. "I promise."

Any guilt Debbie felt was washed away by the thought that she did what a mother had to do, and if need be, she decided that yes, she could do it all again.

Several hours passed peacefully and Debbie's children finally fell asleep. Not long after, two young men gently knocked at what was left of Debbie's door. They were polite and armed only with hand tools. She made them coffee and listened in on their hushed conversation as they repaired the frame and installed new locks.

Debbie was quite stunned when she realized that the firefight she ended wasn't a skirmish between rival drug lords and their hired guns. The men removing evidence in her doorway were members of what she could only describe as a cross between a home owners' association and an armed militia.

They finished up quickly. "We're done. Looks a little nicer than before and the locks are brand new. Otherwise, it's just like nothing ever happened."

"Do I have to pay you?"

"No. It's not like that. Let's just say that someone left a pile of money to the community in his will. Lots of people are going to get new locks around here. Did you talk to your kids? Are they OK?"

Debbie paused to think about it. "Yes. They will be."

The other workman agreed. "They will be because *you* make them feel safe. That's the very first thing a parent should do. My kids would sleep here just fine."

"Thanks. You two are going to make me cry, and I've had enough of that tonight."

"Oh! Hey, no crying. Sorry. Remember that you are not alone. We're going to make sure that this building gets extra protection, and the gentleman who was here earlier told me to give you this. He handed Debbie an envelope. Inside she found an address, three one-hundred-dollar bills, and a note that read:

This is for a better gun.

CHAPTER 2

The Minutemen

Gateway Guns

Charlottesville, VA, 1957

The current gun control debate is primarily focused on a single loaded term: *semiautomatic weapon*. Opinions on the topic tend to be bipolar. Gun folks say, "Buy one before it is too late!" Antigun people ask, "Why in the world would you want one?" It's a fair question. There are any number of whipping boys to take the blame, but underneath it all, the desire to own these weapons has far more to do with honor than paranoia.

There can be no doubt about the media's influence on the gun market. TV and movie stars often elevate guns to cult status. Heroes, whether they like it or not, become firearm salesmen. This effect was innocent enough when it came to John Wayne's trusty six-gun or James Bond's Walther PPK. Nor was it an issue when Clint Eastwood, or rather, Dirty Harry, inadvertently sold countless .44 magnums for Smith & Wesson. Today, however, there must be fifty gun-toting action heroes and villains who pack any number of extra-lethal, jet-black weapons. They no doubt sell millions of semiautomatics for Glock, Colt, and Beretta. The list of manufacturers grows longer every day. These iconic weapons are *gateway guns* that expand and fuel our American gun culture.

Powerful though this force may be, I see the media's influence as an accelerant, not *the* cause. There is an infinitely more subtle and pervasive gun culture experience that sends customers to the gun store, and it has been in play since 1775. I speak, of course, about military service, particularly in times of war.

A great many Americans first experience guns in the armed forces. For example, US Marines are heavily indoctrinated as a corps of supreme riflemen. They memorize and live by the following speech:

The Rifleman's Creed

This is my rifle. There are many like it, but this one is mine.

My rifle is my best friend. It is my life. I must master it as I must master my life.

My rifle, without me, is useless. Without my rifle, I am useless. I must fire my rifle true. I must shoot straighter than my enemy who is trying to kill me. I must shoot him before he shoots me. I will...

My rifle and I know that what counts in this war is not the rounds we fire, the noise of our burst, nor the smoke we make. We know that it is the hits that count. We will hit...

My rifle is human, even as I, because it is my life. Thus, I will learn it as a brother. I will learn its weaknesses, its strength, its parts, its accessories, its sights and its barrel. I will keep my rifle clean and ready, even as I am clean and ready. We will become part of each other. We will...

Before God, I swear this creed. My rifle and I are the defenders of my country. We are the masters of our enemy. We are the saviors of my life.

So be it, until victory is America's and there is no enemy.

The bond between combat veterans and their weapons is bottomless. Many soldiers decide that they cannot do without a civilian version of the weapon they used in battle but had to leave behind. After all, once a soldier always a soldier. Where would the minutemen militia be without a trusty musket to hang over the fireplace?

World Wars I and II, Korea, Vietnam, Afghanistan, and Desert Storm each created a massive crop of returning soldiers in search of a substitute weapon to satisfy that powerful craving. The average veteran's gun collection then trickles down to his or her children and extended family. Imagine what these soldiers teach their sons and daughters about the role of firearms in America.

The current assault rifle craze began in 1945 when military technology ushered in the age of the semiautomatic weapon. The contents of our returning heroes' duffel bags jump-started the market. They brimmed with American, German, Italian and Japanese pistols. Thousands of M-1 carbines, STEN guns, and Nazi MP-40 machine-pistols made it home by hook or by crook. There were quite a few illegal World War II "bring-back" submachine guns floating around the Virginia backwoods...enough to render the sound of automatic fire a yawnable offense.

There were also many De-watted guns. According the National Firearms Act website, a **DEWAT** stands for **DE**activated **WA**r **T**rophy; it was regularly done for servicemen who wished to bring home National Firearms Act restricted weapons as war souvenirs. (The National Firearms Act of 1934 banned fully automatic weapons unless a special license is obtained. It is still in effect today.)

De-watting was also done to World-War-I and World-War-II-era guns imported as surplus by companies like ARMEX International and Interarmco and then sold through the mail in gun and sporting magazines. Those were the glory days before severe restrictions were enacted on these items in 1968. A DEWAT, non-firing though it may be, must now be registered just like a machinegun.

The DEWATs my father and Kyle knew had their firing pins removed and a bore-blocking lead slug rammed into the barrel, but here is the crucial omission: the guns they encountered had no chamber welds. The owner found that a barrel plug can be reamed out, and a firing pin could be made using a lathe and a heat-treated, heavy nail.

My father fondly remembers 1957 and two resurrected, completely illegal guns owned by a dealer from Charlottesville, Virginia. One was a British STEN gun and the other...a Nazi German MP-44 assault rifle. The British submachine gun used nine millimeter parabellum ammunition, which was by no means common in those days. The MP-44 bullets were insanely expensive if obtainable at all. My father, however, was up to the task as he had visited every gun shop from Connecticut to Florida. As fate would have it, he knew a gun dealer in

West Orange, New Jersey, who happened to have a large stock of 7.9 mm kurz ammunition.

"Feeding the MP-44 was rather expensive. I bought several thousand rounds at a time because we tended to run right through our supply, sometimes in a single afternoon. The 44's cyclic rate was much slower than the STEN. It almost sounded as if someone were simply pulling the trigger very fast. It didn't really climb because it was so heavy. I don't remember it ever jamming. It was fairly accurate too. My only complaint with it was that it only took a couple of squirts for the barrel to heat up to about a thousand degrees, and it was easy to forget and burn the hell out of your left hand. The STEN gun was the total opposite of the 44. It let a loud rip that was very distinctive. There was no doubt that somebody was shooting a machinegun. It made us very nervous. It jammed a lot, and its accuracy was miserable. But oh my God, what fun."

MALLORY COLSMANN OF COLSMANN ARMS IN MORGANTOWN, WEST VIRGINIA, SHOWS OFF HER HOT PINK STEN GUN THAT WAS MADE AT COLSMANN ARMS.

I grew up hearing all sorts of gun stories like these. Most were about hunting, but others were pure *Sergeant Rock*, right out of the comic books. There was considerable veteran influence in the Hirsh clan. Uncle Gene told some hardcore tales about fighting the Japanese that gave some graphic color and context to our M-1 Garand, M-1 carbine, and Colt 1911 .45 pistol. My father's less-violent military experience also included several stories about these weapons.

I developed excellent referencing skills for a ten-year-old because I spent endless hours reading my father's copy of *Small Arms of the World*. I looked up the MP-44 and studied it closely. I compared it to everything else in the text. I read that book so many times that it literally disintegrated. I still have the tattered remnants complete with my margin notes that are full of reversed letters and numbers.

I learned that the Nazi "machine-carbine" was an archetype, the very first of the modern assault rifles. The AK-47 and M-16's resemblance to it is impossible to miss. I give the MP-44 rifle, though I never touched one, very special personal status. Like our M-1 Garand and M-1 carbine, it was a gateway gun. It sparked my interest in military history and small arms technology. Ultimately, the MP-44 prompted me to become collector and broker of historic curio and relic military weapons.

Dad will tell you that, "For me, access to those military guns was all in fun. We never really considered their intended purpose. They were just expensive toys. Even in the military, at least for me, the gun stuff was just a bonus. I only got to shoot a few times in basic training, but oh boy did I make the most of it.

"I went through basic training *for doctors*. They barely taught us anything about rifles, and they were positively against giving any of us pistols out of fear that we would accidentally shoot each other. The Dr. Shapiro types from Manhattan and Chicago were terrified of the M-1 rifle, a sentiment widely shared by men who were unusually careful about their hands.

"They'd all heard of 'M-1 thumb.' We had to qualify with the rifle, and there was a rebellion in the ranks about the need to shoot guns in the first place. After all, we were all medical officers. No matter.

We practiced the M-1's operation, including field stripping and how to prevent a thumb injury. You would imagine that surgeons would require about two seconds to learn the whole process, but no. They were definitely special ed in gun class.

"Once on the actual rifle range, I was disappointed that we only had to fire a few clips, and I finished up quickly without any help. The range masters were impressed with my smooth operation and superior accuracy. That sort of thing just didn't happen when training doctors who were considered to be the most difficult recruits."

My father admits, "We doctors do tend to think that we are high and mighty. You have to if you are going to do brain surgery. We were already officers and the drill instructors couldn't really yell at us. Training was more about military protocol than bayonet practice. Anything our drill instructors could do to cut corners was a welcome opportunity for all of us.

"One of the rifle instructors suggested that I move down to the next guy on the firing line to help him shoot. In other words, shoot for him. I did this for at least eight of my colleagues that afternoon, and they were only too happy to let me. I was showing off, I guess, but I was really hot that day. My shoulder was a little sore in the end, but that's a good kind of pain. Later on, I went back to the range with one of the sergeants and shot for those five or six men who failed to qualify. They all scored expert on the second try. The range master thought it was funny as hell and signed off on it. He called us the Dead-eye Doctors."

The other basic training story that stands out in my childhood memories concerns my father crawling under the barbed wire on the infamous Infiltration Course. "Machineguns fire live ammunition just over your head, and instructors set off these enormous firecrackers they called artillery simulators all around us. I did my best to ignore these distractions. You just press yourself as close to mother earth as you can get and slither for your life."

They trained in arid Texas, home to a particularly annoying little burr that sticks to you like Velcro and scratches the skin. It looks like a tiny sea urchin, and the course was coated with them.

Dad always chuckles when he recounts what happened. "Right before our daylight crawl, several of my fellow physicians came up with a plan to save their sensitive skin from the legendary and dreaded Texas burr. They hid out in our tent and taped Kotex pads to their elbows, thighs, and knees. I couldn't believe what I was seeing. They used miles of tape and about fifty dozen pads. You could tell that there was something under their uniforms, but nobody said anything. I never laughed so hard. Of course the protective pads all came loose within the first few yards and wound up around their wrists and ankles.

"The guy in front of me pulled a few out of his shirt and tossed them. Imagine crawling along with bullets snapping inches above you, sharp wire everywhere, and explosions going off. I was making good time and thinking about how my platoon mates were a bunch of pussies, and there, right in front of my chin, was a Kotex pad."

Unlike just about everyone else in my father's platoon—and perhaps in the entire fourteen hundred doctors in training—Captain Hirsh was thoroughly enjoying himself, at least until their tallest man freaked out and stood straight up into the machine fire.

As it turned out, the guns were fired electrically and instantly cut off with the flick of a switch. "Everyone had to stop because he was tangled in the wire and couldn't get back down. Nor could he easily be reached as the wire was too tall to step over. The instructors had to crawl out there themselves to cut the wire and push him through.

"We didn't have any problems on the night crawl. The machinegun tracers were actually awe inspiring. The whole course is quite wide. Waves of troops go all at once. Getting through takes a while, and you have time to notice the sounds that bullets make. Under the wire and under fire, you can hear the rounds crack and echo simultaneously. I wished I could just roll over on my back, hang out, and watch the show."

My father did his tour of duty at the Pentagon and never heard a shot fired in anger. "The closest I ever got to combat surgery took place in San Antonio, Texas, at the end of basic training. They wanted us to practice stabilizing wounded soldiers. The lesson was more than brutal as they substituted goats for men."

The doomed animals were given some sort of crude anesthesia and then shot in the thigh. "They brought them in one by one through a large door in the back of the huge room we were in. It was like a pole-building barn with a packed dirt floor. There were rows of stainless steel tables and lights so that we could really see what we were doing as we started IVs and tried to stop the bleeding."

They were expected to keep their goats alive for twenty minutes.

"It seemed like only seconds before the training officer blew a whistle and announced, 'Time's up!' If your goat was still alive, they checked off your name. Then they just dismissed us, and we walked out with the goats still half alive on the tables. We formed up in our ranks quite uncharacteristically without a single mumble or complaint. We could hear a muffled pop, pop, pop of a pistol as we marched away."

The age of the machinegun fun came to an abrupt end for the Hirsh family in 1960. The MP-44 and STEN gun just disappeared when the gun dealer they belonged to went out of business. If he managed to hang onto the guns for another eight years, he might have properly registered them in 1968 when there was a general amnesty declared for illegally held automatic weapons.

Nobody knows how many people stashed away their unregistered machineguns rather than chance having their weapons confiscated by the federal government. To this day illegal machineguns regularly show up in grandma's post grandpa garage sale.

Machineguns can still be privately owned in most states when properly licensed by the Bureau of Alcohol Tobacco and Firearms. There are approximately 250,000 tradable guns in the system and countless thousands more that are licensed to law enforcement. An MP-44 on this legal market might bring as much as $25,000.

Of course, you can get a semiautomatic version of just about anything for a fraction of the pesos. Colt Firearms was the first to market a semiautomatic-only version of the M-16 in the mid-1960s. They were pricey items, but Vietnam vets and police departments snapped them up like hotcakes. Suddenly every major manufacturer of military small arms offered civilian versions of their flagship weapons on the American market. Ruger, Colt, Armalite, Universal, Springfield Armory, SIG, Iver Johnson, Heckler and Koch, Sterling, Bushmaster, FN, Beretta, Norinco, Howa, CETME, Steyr, Leader, Valmet, and Israeli Military Industries sold hundreds of thousands of weapons in the United States without complaint for close to thirty years.

The semiautomatic AK-47 was one of the last rifles to hit the American market. Its arrival in the early 1980s caused quite a sensation. The very idea that an actual AK-47 could exist in the United States seemed a stretch. In a move I can't begin to imagine these days, the BATF signed off on their importation. The government's attitude was that these rifles were destined for recreational use, so why worry? At first, AK rifles were very expensive, and the ammo was hard to find, but that didn't seem to matter. Vietnam vets could buy the gun that opposed them. Prices for the gun and ammunition fell as demand increased. Soon anyone could afford an AK or SKS rifle and a ton of ammo to go with it.

There is one other sales accelerant that came into play about twenty-five years ago in an attempt to counter the military semiautomatic's popularity. Assault weapons became a political *and simultaneously* a moral issue. Either one of these might be survivable, but together they were thought to be a knock-out punch.

Rather than shaming gun owners into wrapping their rifles around a tree or dumping them at sea, people ran out to buy more of them. The first President Bush banned assault rifle importation, but people could still bring in assault-rifle-parts kits and assemble them here. These duplicate weapons are referred to as clones. Then the assault weapons ban under Bill Clinton identified certain traits that, taken in sum, make an assault rifle what it is. In most cases cosmetic changes, such as removing the flash hider and bayonet lug, were all that was needed to purify the weapon and get it back on the market.

The firearms industry responded to the ban on assault rifle importation by building factories here in the United States. Most of these are located in the Northeast, but recently there has been a gun company exodus from that hostile territory to the gun welcoming Southern states.

The Clinton gun ban expired in 2004, and bayonet lugs came back into fashion, until the Sandy Hook school shooting and the Colorado movie massacre prompted President Obama to try one more time to freeze the pool of assault weapons and register the ones already in the public arsenal. He failed and set off an epic buying frenzy, perhaps the largest of all time.

We were all convinced that the door on military-style weapons was about to close forever, and soon we would be fighting just to keep what we have. (This *is* the case in Connecticut and New York.) The base cost for an AR-15 or AK-47 doubled overnight. Ammunition disappeared from the shelves at Wal-Mart, Gander Mountain, and Cabela's. The armed and nervous bought tens of thousands of high-capacity magazines as well. The National Rifle Association signed up one million new members in less than a year.

I was not immune to the angst, but there was only one gun that I really wanted. And predictably it brought me back to my original gateway gun.

I was looking for the right piece to be my capper—the one to end my collecting so that I could focus back on other interests. I already had one or more of everything worth having, except for an MP-44.

A semiautomatic version of the MP-44 built on an old Nazi-parts kit costs about five grand. There were only a few hundred of them made, so that was out of the question. Just as I was about to give up my quest, German Sports Guns released an exact replica of the MP-44 in .22 long-rifle caliber. It feels for all the world just like the real thing. Best of all, it costs peanuts.

My replica MP-44 had to pass one test. I sat my father down and said, "I am going to blindfold you and then hand you a rifle. I want you to tell me what it is just by its feel." He was intrigued by the experiment and quickly identified every one of our guns without looking. Then I handed him my new MP-44 .22.

"Wow, this one is really heavy. Obviously it's an assault rifle. It isn't an M-16 or AK. It feels like one of the older ones." He found the cocking-handle and pulled it back. "It reminds me of the old MP-44."

He removed the blindfold. "Oh My God! it's an MP-44! How in the world did you get this?"

I told him about how the gun market is flooded with .22 caliber clones of just about any military rifle you would care to name. I call this trend "the new rimfire reality." These rifles lack the full-automatic option, and they fire just about the smallest bullet there is, but we both agreed that the weapon's feel was the most important thing.

These little plinkers can be shot on indoor pistol ranges and places where you don't want to make a ton of noise and scare the neighbors. Kids can easily manage these rifles, and the low price of ammunition allows them to put in some serious practice.

Rimfire military style rifles are the finest examples of dedicated gateway guns and will no doubt only become more popular as the price of real assault rifle ammunition continues to rise. My new MP-44 is more toy than tactical. But it channels my childhood, and that is good enough for me.

UNCLE GENE'S CARBINE

Okinawa: April, 1945

Marine Lieutenant Eugene Folks checked his carbine and began a fifty-yard low crawl to the edge of the ridge. He trailed a commo wire that stretched back to his mortar platoon. The battle raged around him, but he was intent on one particular problem that was spraying bullets just inches over his head. The enemy machinegun was close and fired from a well-hidden bunker somewhere across the draw. It covered the only avenue off the ridge and into the Japanese defenses.

"My company was pinned down, and I was just wait'n for that goddamn Jap mortar and artillery to cut us up. You could count on the little bastards to drop 'em right in your back pocket. I knew we had about two minutes to solve the problem and get the hell outa there. That's why I went out there, myself."

The emperor's soldiers had indeed noticed the opportunity. There was no time to be cautious. Lieutenant Folks took cover behind a rock that proved to be just a bit too small. His right leg from the knee down was exposed.

Where are you, Nambu? I'll give you something to shoot at. He lifted his head to invite its fire and saw the muzzle flash of the gun that so wanted him. "There you are," Gene muttered. He called for fire, and his men responded.

Uncle Gene's war stories painted a complete picture of the battlefield, including many references to the sounds of the various weapons trying to kill him. Apparently, Japanese Type 92 machineguns have a distinctive report: Tac-tac-tac. Gene described it as a woodpecker. The gunner fired at Gene's head and missed, but he saw the leg and attempted to dial his weapon in on it. The mortar bombs falling in front of his bunker made it a difficult shot.

"I was so intent on killing those Japs that I didn't even really notice getting hit." Gene said that the 6.5 mm bullet passed right through his calf. "I thought it was a centipede bite. I was more scared of them than the goddamn Nips. I frantically looked for the bug, and I was a little relieved to find it was just a bullet hole. That I could live with.

"My mortars couldn't get the job done. We needed the bazooka and flamethrower team. The commo line got cut, so I had to crawl all the way back to get them."

The way Uncle Gene tells the story, the pain wasn't worth his attention. Knowing him as we do, this seems plausible. "I knew I was in for it when that woodpecker stopped tapping. They tried to rush us. I rolled over in time to see a Jap soldier take aim at me, but he missed." Gene put two 110-grain bullets in the center of the man's chest. He fell forward to reveal the next soldier coming up the slope, and again, a precise shot dropped his enemy. Gene said that he couldn't tell where "Jap after goddamn Jap" was coming from, but come they did from many directions. He fired back coolly, but he quickly used up the magazines in his pockets and the pouch on his rifle stock.

"There was one Nip that I know I hit at least twice, but he kept banging away at me anyway. That was just my sloppy shooting. I didn't have time to aim. I musta gut shot him." As for the rest of the story, Gene pulled his Colt 1911 .45, fought on, and lived to tell us about it for the next sixty years. They put a Band-aid on his wound, and he rejoined his unit.

It took Gene about five years to calm down after the war. He wasn't burned out or suffering from PTSD, and despite his use of racial epithets when telling his war stories, I know that he bore no malice for his former enemies. He was proud of his service, and people always honored him and thanked him for it, particularly at the end of his life. He just needed to process the experience. By 1950, his exploits had become a sort of script and his stories the stuff of legends. But always, underneath the bravado, I suspect he was frustrated by the reality that his battles would never completely leave him alone.

Gene Folks was a top-notch engineer who worked very closely with my grandfather at Lock Joint Pipe. He was also a long-time, close family friend who taught my dad how to play the guitar. As a result, I play too. Eventually Gene and Pop had a falling out, and Pop challenged Gene to a fist fight. Gene laughed and said, "I killed a hundred Japs a day. I'll take you apart."

Gene left Lock Joint and went to work for a rival company. I didn't see him often when I was a kid. He told me the war stories when I was very young, but even as a nine-year-old, I wanted more information about the weapons he used.

He was delighted to tell me. To paraphrase: The Thompson was too heavy. The Garand was fine but too long. A .45 was all he really needed. And above all, his carbine was the best choice for jungle fighting.

Gene was great with kids. My father tells me that he rode around the farm with his "uncle" who taught him all about mortar platoon tactics. The content was rather bloodthirsty by today's standards, but to my dad, Gene was just like any other superhero who beat up on bad guys.

"You see that ridge? Now think about three Nambu machineguns shooting right at you. Here's whatcha do." Other quotes that stuck with us to this day include: "I heard something, so I flipped around and shot up the jungle right behind me. A big fat Jap rolled right out of the bush."

Another favorite: "I woke up and saw a Jap officer kill one of my guys with a Samurai sword. I always slept with my .45 tied to my hand. He came right for me screaming like a son of a bitch, so I flipped off the safety and dropped him."

We have Uncle Gene's carbine and .45 today. He wasn't going to "lift" them, but his supply sergeant stuck them in his duffel bag without his knowing. At least, that was Gene's excuse. At the last family picnic with him, he told the old war stories, but this time he added something else.

As I think back on it, I wonder if Gene had deliberately waited sixty years to unleash his surprise. He wanted us all together and made a lot of phone calls to make sure that we had three generations at the gathering. Gene insisted in particular that my father and his cousin, Doug Hirsh, were in attendance.

I remember thinking that Uncle Gene didn't tell the stories all that well. He'd lost the marine spark. He was really rather sad, but his pride rang through. When he finished, he had a sudden second wind. "Come here, men," he demanded like an officer. He waddled over to his car, a great big Lincoln Continental, and opened the trunk. "Here is the carbine." He reached in and handed Doug the carbine-sized package. "And here is the .45." He gave my father the shoebox package. "These have never been opened since 1945. Go ahead men. Why don't you open them now?" He was smug and handed over his pocketknife.

The carbine was packed in a heavy, brown, waxed paper sleeve, still taped just the way it had been when he left Guam in 1945. There was a note scribbled on it, but I do not know what it said. I wish I knew what became of the packaging. From a collector's standpoint, these weapons have a great story and a unique twist. So long as they remained unopened, their value was limitless. Naturally we had them open on the spot. The Inland Motors carbine was in good condition outwardly, but its internals were well worn. It was still reliable and accurate even with the dented magazine. We thought it a fitting tribute to shoot Uncle Gene's carbine right after his funeral service.

We have yet to shoot the .45, which we salted away deep behind many locks.

I saw Uncle Gene one last time before he peacefully passed away. He wasn't interested in having a Jack Daniels with me, a sign that he didn't have long to live. True to form, he told me a war story. I have presented it here. He praised his weapons with a reverence that bordered on faith. He groused about his Thompson again. It was still too heavy. He threw it away. Oh, but his carbine…it was mythically accurate in his hands. So good, in fact, that just like a pool ball banked into the corner pocket, he could careen tracers into caves where a direct shot could not go.

So…when I think carbine or .45 the first image in my head is of Uncle Gene in the jungle. The fact that we have his weapons is of historical and emotional value. This is the nexus of gun and family. By the way, though semiautomatic and capable of accepting high capacity magazines, the M-1 carbine is legal to own just about everywhere.

We buried Gene last year. I recited Shakespeare's "band of brothers" speech from *Henry the Fifth* at the service, and the marine honor guard took him the rest of the way, with all of us heartbroken and somber behind.

M-1 Thumb

Mason Dixon Rifle Club, 1990

The M-1 Garand served America's soldiers from 1936 to 1957. My example has served our family for more than sixty years. I first shot it when I was ten years old, but after that we rarely used it. The Garand was more of a collectable than a practical rifle. All that changed in the late nineties when I took up competitive rifle shooting.

The Civilian Marksmanship Program (CMP) has been around for more than one hundred years. It was created by the US Congress as part of the War Department Appropriations Act of 1903. The Office of the Director of Civilian Marksmanship (DCM) is responsible for implementing this nationwide program. The underlying purpose was to create a nation of skilled riflemen who could dominate the battlefield with their superior shooting skills.

CMP highpower rifle matches are as close to military training as a civilian can get. Competitors use American service rifles, such as the 1903 Springfield, M-1 Garand, M-14 (The civilian version is called the M1A), and M-16 (AR-15). The national matches at Camp Perry, Ohio were first held in 1907. They are described as the "World Series of the shooting sports."

I participated in this program for ten years. I built on my childhood summer camp training and learned to shoot a high-powered rifle effectively from the standing (offhand), sitting, and prone positions.

I rediscovered an acute awareness of my breathing, sight picture, and trigger control. My scores improved, and I climbed the ladder from marksman to sharpshooter quite quickly. These skills spilled over into my hunting and recreational shooting.

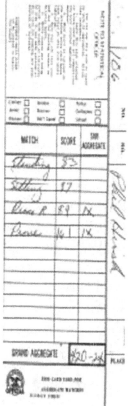

HERE WE SEE A LEFT HANDED COMPETITOR FIRING AN M-1A RIFLE WHICH IS THE SEMIAUTOMATIC ONLY VERSION OF THE M-14. NOTE THE SHOOTING JACKET. THE SCORE CARD IS AN ARTIFACT FROM MY EARLY COMPETITIVE SHOOTING DAYS.

All shooters can benefit from this program. Let's face it—without a bench rest, 99 percent of us would be completely lost. Remember that tiny groups fired from a sandbagged rest reveal the accuracy of the gun, not the ability of the shooter.

Picture yourself as a competitor at a DCM match. You've got your padded shooting jacket on; you're looking the part—you blend. There are fifteen shooters in your relay. You will fire a total of fifty rounds over the course of four events. The fifteen targets look a long way off. In the confusion of loading and firing, it is easy to get mixed up and cross-fire on the wrong target. Be careful! Your opponent keeps the best ten, and you lose ten points.

Traditionally, DCM matches are fired at three distances: two hundred, three hundred, and six hundred yards. There are very few rifle ranges that can provide this course of fire. Most of the matches I shot in used reduced-sized targets to simulate greater distances. At Mason Dixon Rifle Club, all stages were shot at two hundred yards.

THE AUTHOR'S WIFE PREPARES FOR THE SITTING, RAPID-FIRE RIFLE MATCH EVENT. NOTE THE SAFETY BLOCK THAT IS LOCKED IN THE ACTION AT ALL TIMES BETWEEN THE ORDERS TO OPEN FIRE AND CEASE FIRE. THE M-1 GARAND ISN'T A PRACTICAL RIFLE FOR ANNE'S LEVEL OF EXPERIENCE, BUT THE AR-15 WORKS WELL FOR HER.

One cannot help but observe that safety is everyone's first priority. If safe-gun handling were an Olympic event, these target shooters would be in the medals. There is always a range master who watches over the scene. Our guy was a retired Marine Corps Vietnam veteran who could summon up his old persona and be that rifle range officer of old. He barked, but nobody minded.

It all began with his calling out, "Shooters! You have two minutes to prepare." There are several last-moment things to check. We make final adjustments to our sights and focus spotting scopes. One's rifle sling must be properly set, and ammunition should be easy reach. Finally, I always tried to close my eyes and take a few deep breaths as I waited for the command to open fire.

"Shooters, rise!" All competitors have to start each event standing with a clip of bullets in one hand and an unloaded weapon in the other. When the order is given, we drop into position and *then* load our rifles.

The range master calls out, "All ready on the left! All ready on the right! All ready on the firing line! Commence...Firing!"

In the first event, you have to shoot standing offhand without benefit of a sling. We fire ten rounds in ten minutes. Each cartridge is loaded one at a time. This event is almost leisurely. The spotting scope is crucial as it keeps the shooter informed of every point and so indicates how the sights should be adjusted to make each shot an X.

In the second event, the shooter has to stand and wait for the command to commence firing. He or she then assumes the sitting position to fire ten shots *in sixty seconds* with a mandatory reload. It is a struggle to quickly get into an effective sitting position. I always fired two shots and then reloaded the next eight. As I did this, I listened to my spotter calling the sight correction. "Come up two clicks, right one click!"

The next ten shots come in the standing-to-prone event. Again, there is a mandatory reload. You have seventy seconds to fire ten shots and score one hundred points. The sound of fifteen .30-caliber rifles firing one hundred fifty shots in less than a minute is awe inspiring.

The final event is fired from the prone position. The shooter has twenty minutes to fire twenty rounds, each loaded one at a time. This sounds easy, but the bull's-eye, or X ring, for this event is about the size of an Oreo cookie. After a few minutes your back begins to hurt, and your supporting hand goes numb. Most shooters rush right through this event, which counts for 40 percent of the overall score.

My first DCM M-1 Garand match was a wake-up call. I scored three hundred fifty out of five hundred possible points. I didn't really know the course of fire, and it was all a bit overwhelming. I settled down. The competitors were friendly, and they helped me get my positions right and rifle tuned. I bought a shooting jacket and a shooter's mitt. My scores went up to four hundred and hovered there. I ended the season as first marksman. I quickly realized that in order to move up the ladder, I would need an M-1A (the civilian version of the military M-14 rifle), which improved my score by twenty points the very first time I used it.

Garand devotees may object, but I have to say that the M-1A is a far better weapon on the target range than its parent.

Since the Garand is heavier than an M-14, it is better for doing curls. One needs upper-body strength to be a Garand master. We put up with the weight because the M-1 rifle is about history, invention, and independence. It represents a free people's belief that a soldier's life is too precious to arm him with anything less than an ass kicker in a firefight. The M-1 Garand did that decisively for twenty years. I find it ironic that my college-age son loves the M-1 and likes to give his friends a go with it. They all walk away saying that they have to have one.

It's that cool.

I have early memories of the M-1. My dad used to take it out in the yard—at the farm—and bump fire the thing which for those of you who don't know involves pulling the trigger so fast that one can rip through the entire magazine in about a second. The noise and flash made quite an impression. I was hooked on guns at five years of age by the blazing, blasting eight *cabooms* and one *ping* of Dad's Garand.

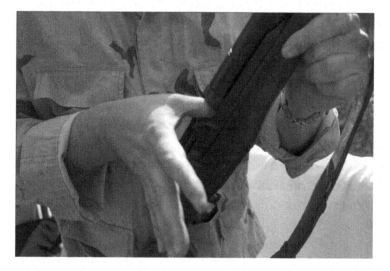

THIS IS WHAT M-1 THUMB LOOKS LIKE. THE TRICK IS TO HOLD THE BOLT OPEN WITH THE SIDE OF YOUR HAND WHILE PRESSING THE MAGAZINE FOLLOWER DOWN ENOUGH TO RELEASE THE BOLT.

Good, old Dad used to scare the hell out of me by sticking his thumb down into the mag well to release the bolt. If you do this incorrectly, the bolt will slam home and give you a bad case of M-1 thumb. He somehow always got it out of there in one smooth motion. Obviously I could not see that he was holding the action open with the side of his hand until he got his thumb clear. Eventually I learned the trick, and I used to scare my kids too (more tradition).

Don't get M-1 thumb at the range. People will openly empathize with your considerable agony—and it is agony—beyond "Ow! That smarts!" But inside, they may well be laughing at you. I can't think of another weapon that can actually bite its user. So practice in private and then show off.

Those who know how to fire America's service rifles experience a unique history lesson every time they go to the range. In a modern armory full of AR-15 and AK-47 style weapons, it seems impossible that the M-1 was the predominant infantry weapon from 1936 until 1945 when the first assault rifle made its début in Nazi hands. General George Patton described the rifle as the "best battle implement ever devised."

The seemingly ancient M-1 Garand lacks firepower, but the full power thirty caliber round it fires can drop anything from a moose to Big Foot. Best of all, the Garand is legal to own in all fifty states because its magazine can only hold eight rounds, and thus it is not an assault rifle.

THE FULDA GAP

West Germany, 1956

At dawn, a company of elite Soviet reconnaissance troops debussed from their personnel carriers four hundred yards in front of Captain Hewitt Jones's observation post. The peace talks had broken down, and the most experienced officers were sent out into the Fulda Gap no man's land to await "an incident." Hewitt was an experienced officer with two previous wars to hone his instincts, and he recognized the sound of enemy tanks stacking up across the border. By first light, he could smell their exhaust.

Jones received his orders at the fire direction center where slide rules outnumber rifles by a factor of ten to one. The rules of engagement were reviewed in detail. Restraint was the watch word.

"Good luck men," the colonel said. "God help us all. Dismissed. Captain Jones? Will you remain behind?"

"Yes sir."

The colonel waited for the rest of the officers to sidle out. "Here we go again, Huey. I need that steely nerve of yours one more time. That's why I'm sending you to the hottest spot. We've been through two wars together, and I know better than anybody that you are a fine artillerist. I don't know what to think of these other officers, but I trust you to follow orders and relay accurately what you see happening. God knows what the Soviets will pull. It could always come as a feint, or they could come at us hell bent with everything they have. You've got the best observation post. Don't bother with heavy weapons. We'll support you."

"Yes sir. Understood." Jones paused to offer his old friend a parting handshake. "Perhaps cooler heads will prevail, John."

"Sure thing. Cooler heads. Lots of those around. See you soon, Huey. We'll be listening for your call."

Once in the observation post things seemed rather less than optimistic. Jones studied the enemy through his spotting scope, "What do *you* think, Sergeant?"

"I didn't think they were going to stop. They're just sitting there like they actually want to draw fire."

"They are definitely on our turf, now. No question." Jones said flatly, "I think the Eighth Guards are serious this time." He surveyed his enemy and referenced his map. "They're forming a skirmish line. You called it, Bob. They are daring us to shoot."

Sergeant Smith considered the big picture. "Nobody else is shooting. No airstrikes, either."

NATO command knew that the Fulda Gap was the most likely line of attack, and they put a great deal of time and resources to block any assault. The camouflaged observation posts that dotted the valley blended perfectly with their surroundings. Captain Jones and his riflemen were dug into the top of a low, rocky knoll. The artillery observer's position was at the extreme right of the bunker and sat above several well concealed embrasures that extended for twenty-five yards to his left. The terrain to the front was devoid of cover—a perfect killing field. The only way into their bunker was through a hatch on the reverse slope. In the event of a bug out, a soldier might be able to use the ravines to high tail it back the main line of resistance. The only other exit was a hatch in the observer's overhead cover through which a signal pistol could be fired.

Jones had a panoramic view of the entire front. The tools of his trade, spotting scope, communications, and map table were all in readiness. His riflemen prepared to defend the Observation post. They stacked BAR magazines and Garand eight shot clips. The designated grenadier laid out his M7 grenade launcher and five antitank shaped charge grenades.

Like all good soldiers, they groused as they worked. "Now we'll find out if all this digging was worth it."

"Take it from me. The Japs didn't make them this good at Okinawa."

"This place is more like the Alamo, and we all know what happened to them."

Sergeant Smith tapped his CO's shoulder. "Captain, the colonel is on the command net for you."

Hewitt took the handset and gave his call sign. "You hit the nail on the head, sir. They chose my doorstep, but it's just a recon unit right now." He listened intently. "Yes sir, they're up to something. I will advise. Out." He turned to his platoon sergeant, "Bob, here's the news. I'm supposed to wait for them to fire first."

"They're on the move. Give them three minutes, and they'll be right on top of us."

"That's right, and stepping on me is the same thing as shooting me. Let's take the bait."

Jones looked through his binoculars at the Soviet infantry as they unknowingly closed on his miniature fortress. He formed his strategy. *First I'm going to kill those armored vehicles. Then I'll airburst a couple.* The handset was his weapon of choice. He calmly relayed preregistered coordinates and fire concentrations to the mortars and artillery that depended on him to be their eyes.

"Those guys out there are cooked meat."

The sergeant replied, "Not if they don't start shootin'."

Jones made a command decision. "Well, you're right about that. Remember the Revolutionary War? The shot heard round the world? Well, the Redcoats are coming. Let's plug one and see what happens. Private Hamm!"

"Yes, sir!"

"Kindly do that rifle thing you do so well so we can get this war started."

Private First Class Arty Hamm studied the enemy through the scope of his M-1D sniper rifle. They came on at a trot, stopping every few yards to take a knee and scan ahead. His mind raced, but his breathing slowed. *Officers first, radio second, then heavy weapons. So hard to choose.*

Arty took careful aim at an officer and his radio operator. A third soldier with them unfolded a map. His rhythmic breathing was tied to the slack on a trigger he had pulled thousands of times.

The first shot of the day killed the officer with a three-hundred-fifty-yard perfect hit to center mass. The radio operator died a split second later. The soldier with the map was actually hit between the eyes. The mix of adrenaline and sheer marksmanship flowed through every shot. The eight consecutive blasts triggered a nervous burst from the BAR gunner. The advancing infantry saw the muzzle flashes and adjusted their assault to meet them.

One hundred AK-47s barked back as the Soviet troops bounded forward in textbook style under the cover of their roughly aimed suppressive fire and supported by their battle taxis' machineguns. The Americans shot back, but the enemy had undeniable fire superiority and rode their advantage.

"I think we started it. I'm calling this in."

Jones advised command that he was under fire, requested an artillery adjustment, and then dropped the handset to pick up his M-1. He aimed carefully and squeezed the trigger. The rifle bucked, and the target fell, but the incoming fire rattled his marksmanship and negated the M-1's accuracy advantage.

The Soviet troops delivered a hail of lead completely disproportionate to their numbers. Jones flashed back to his first experience with this kind of offensive firepower. He was a young corporal in Germany, 1945. A platoon of Hitler youth mounted a raid and shot up his convoy. They had machine pistols, but the most common firearm among the dead was the MP-44 assault rifle. Jones collected one of these stamped-and-pressed game changers, and he planned to mail it home piece by piece. Much to his regret, however, he lost it in a poker game.

Six years later, while serving in Korea, he was the lone survivor of a predawn human wave attack where most of the enemy soldiers were armed with Russian PPSh burp guns. The barrage of incoming rounds chewed everything around him to pieces, and the accompanying staccato fixed his men in their positions. They were all killed or captured, but he was overlooked. Before he rotated back to the states, he stashed a PPS-43 in his duffel bag.

Jones had no intention of a repeat Korean experience. For perhaps a minute, the war was just a skirmish between a couple hundred troops and a few personnel carriers. Both sides could have said, "Sorry about that," and gone home.

Nothing escalates a battle more than an artillery barrage, but the first salvo of the fight was drastically off target. Three of the four infantry carriers were put of action, but their passengers ranging ahead were relatively unscathed.

Jones called for a correction and additional mortar support.

Sergeant Smith said, "They're getting a little close for all that, Captain."

The surviving BTR fired a heavy weapon directly into the OP. Jones and his radio operator were pinned to the floor and mauled by fragments as seven-hundred-grain tracer rounds ripped away the overhead cover's supports. The roof collapsed, probably saving their lives by sealing the aperture from any more point blank devastation.

A rifle grenade fired from the observation post sailed like a perfectly thrown football to blow a molten metal hole above the personnel carrier's frontal vision block. A second grenade, fired only seconds later, hit between the driver and gunner's positions. There were explosions inside the vehicle. It stopped with a lurch and began to smoke.

Jones could squeeze his head and shoulders through the signal pistol hatch, and didn't need his binoculars to see the enemy's progress. They were crawling around in his perimeter, and his boys couldn't depress their rifles enough to shoot them as they scrambled from rock to rock.

Hewitt held his breath, waiting for the claymore mines to even the odds. Most were tripped within seconds of one another as enemy troops tried to take cover only to find the next claymore had gotten there first. Finally, the mortars Jones had called landed danger close. The Soviet recon unit ceased to exist.

Sergeant Smith checked his men. "Sound off!" The troopers responded, almost cheerfully, as they reloaded their weapons.

Private Hamm and his telescopic sight had the best view of the developing situation. "Captain, look at the tree line!"

Countless personnel carriers broke out and advanced in line abreast. The first tanks to attack that day rolled out behind them. They fired wildly as they sped across the open ground. Jones could hear their shells pass only feet over his dugout. The accuracy of Soviet fire was abysmal, but the sheer volume itself was more than intimidating.

Jones huddled with Sergeant Smith. "Captain, the land line's dead. We still have radio."

The ground shook with explosion after explosion as a rolling barrage swept a corridor for the mechanized brigade. The fragment tornado clawed closer to the observation post. Everyone in the fort hunkered down and hoped that God was still on their side. Jones accepted his demise. *Now I get to find out if I used up all my luck in Korea.*

The shells passed over, and Jones was able to raise his head through the observation hatch. He had no maps to reference, but the Soviet formation was impossible to miss. Jones adjusted fire and succeeded in destroying the carriers and tanks before they could cross the field, but the surviving infantry carried on. They had farther to run in the open then the dead men strewn in front of Hewitt's outpost, but this wave was three full companies strong and four more companies after that. The mortars, 105s, and 155 mm howitzers continued to thin them out, but here and there platoons survived intact.

The soldiers under Jones's command were all life long shooters from the deep South. They understood how to lead a target and adjust for the wind, but the thing that made them truly deadly was the fact that they loved their M-1 Garand rifles and were supremely confident in their shooting skills. Arty opened fire six hundred yards. The rest of the riflemen raked over the infantry well outside the AK's effective range.

The Soviet's opened fire at three hundred yards. Most didn't seem to know what they were facing and simply fired to the front. Ninety-nine percent was wasted effort, but two Americans were killed as random rounds found the embrasures. The rest of the men forced their courage to the sticking place and continued to fire clip after clip. Miraculously, as the Soviets closed in, their fire largely went high.

Jones was still making steel rain with the radio, but the 105s protecting his position went silent. The 155s, operating from farther back still, voiced their opposition, but there were too few to stop another wave.

Hewitt recognized the signs. "Sergeant, we're going to be over run. This is hopeless. You and the men bug out."

Smith ignored his CO. Eight M-1s still resisted. They fired steadily. The telltale *pings* of the ejecting clips chimed up and down the firing line. The rifles ripple fired, like a broadside from the *USS Constitution*. But they had no visible effect on the assault, and Jones could summon only a few 81 mm mortars in their final defense. Two squads of Soviet infantry survived the mad dash and reached pistol range.

"Time to go, men! Get the hell out of here!"

Jones stood up in the hatch, exposing himself to three enemy soldiers who were surprised by his sudden appearance. He took an extra split second to hold the rifle firmly as he leaned into the shot. Looking over the sights and aiming low, he dumped his eight rounds and killed all three men. Then a grenade exploded, wounding him badly in the right shoulder. He dropped back through the hatch, but without two hands to maneuver his Garand, he was unable to keep the long rifle.

Hewitt's men bugged out, but rather than running for home, they took up positions on the crest of their bunker. With bayonets fixed and the Southern soldiers' Rebel yell, they tried to shoot it out at point-blank range, but their Garands were hopelessly outmatched by the Soviets' assault rifles. They responded with the last of their hand grenades, but they were quickly flanked and had no hope of survival.

Captain Jones drew his .45 and pulled his riddled body though the signal hatch. He crawled forward, looking for one last target. Blood loss blurred his vision, but he could hear a nearby enemy soldier shouting orders. Hewitt propped himself up against a boulder, dropped his pistol, and reached for his hand grenade.

Sergeant Federov huddled behind a rock and called for his radioman, but he lay headless in the field. He looked for an officer, but thanks to Private Hamm's scoped M-1 and NATO artillery, they too were gone. Federov realized that he was in command but decided to sit tight and wait for the second wave. He looked back for this relief but saw only scores of smoldering hulks and the remaining armor retreating behind a smoke screen. He looked for his air support, but the low-flying planes were headed in the wrong direction.

Federov made the sign of the cross and called out for his men to retreat. He waved them past and acted as their rear guard. Once alone, he mumbled a few words to God, dropped his AK-47 and slowly stood up with his hands in the air. He glanced downward and was shocked to see Hewitt with a grenade in one hand and the pin in the other.

"Nyet! Nyet! America! America!"

Captain Hewitt Jones was on his third and last war. He was hardened to death, even of his own men, and he gave himself no less quarter. He was beyond reason and past all hope, but the last shred of his martial instinct found its way to his right hand, and he held down the grenade's spoon.

Federov was ruled by his own instincts, but unlike the veteran at his feet, his were tempered by a different manual. He lowered his hands and reached for his enemy.

Sergeant Smith stepped up behind Federov in time to see him disarm the pineapple and drop it in Hewitt's lap. He tapped the Soviet on the shoulder with the flat of his fixed bayonet.

"Stand up. Hands on your head. That's a good commie."

Federov smiled broadly, nodded profusely, and did as he was told. He held one hand in the air and gestured for permission to reach into his hip pocket.

"What have you got? Slowly now."

Federov produced two items. The first was a combat dressing that he intended to use on Hewitt. The second item was a tiny rosary which he hung on Smith's outstretched bayonet.

"Well, I'll be damned."

Hewitt was unaware of the gesture. "Where'd the war go, Bob?"

"It ran away to where it came from I suspect."

"The men?"

"The men had the good sense to not let themselves get flanked. They decided to leave it to the three of us. It's just you, me and your Russian doctor."

"Very well. More than enough. Before I pass out, do me a favor."
"I'll let your wife know you're going to be OK. Don't worry."
"Yeah, that's good. She'll like that. But there's something else."
"Anything. Make it quick. It's time to go."
"Sure, just grab me one of those rifles and drop it in the mail."

THE SKS RIFLE (TOP) HAS A LIMITED MAGAZINE CAPACITY OF TEN ROUNDS. IT CAN BE MODIFIED TO TAKE HIGH CAPACITY MAGAZINES LIKE THE AK BELOW IT. BUT, IN ITS PUREST FORM AND WITHOUT BAYONET, IT IS EVEN LEGAL IN CALIFORNIA.

MR. NUMBER'S SKS

Morgantown, West Virginia, 1992

Aside from my own stupidities, I can list the unsafe shooting situations I have seen on one hand. Two involved SKS rifles. I have to list the first victim as one of those coworker friends that you lose track of when you trade professions. He was a super-nice fellow who had a few guns of his own. He taught math, and I taught English. So we were kinda opposites by nature. The second event involved a pair of total strangers who put my entire town at risk. I damn near had to shoot them.

POINT-BLANK EFFECT

The word *militia* conjures up different images with different people. I recall that back in the early 1990s militia movements were springing up all over the place. A few of my fellow teacher friends and I decided that we should form our own unit but with a difference. We weren't serious. It was all a weird spoof for us. Our logo involved a camo-clad militia guy riding a giant bazooka. It was a trifle obscene, especially because it was going off. Bottom line, though, we were absolutely serious about our gun rights.

Behind every bit of sarcasm exists a tiny modicum of truth. We did have a lot of guns, including SKS rifles. We made this the standard issue weapon for the West Virginia Free Militia. Naturally, a well-regulated militia needs to practice marksmanship. The ten of us gathered at the range for our first semiannual training day.

We designed a course of fire where we could run and gun or "rattle battle" at various silhouette targets set at twenty-five, fifty, one hundred and two hundred yards. We did have safety in mind, and while advancing station to station, the gun had to be empty and the action open.

All went well until Mr. Numbers made his run. He had a bit of trouble at the last station.

He was supposed to shoot offhand from the one-hundred-yard line to the two-hundred-yard line, but his target blew lose in the wind. Rather than suspend fire and then go back out to fix things, he chose to run all the way to the fallen target. He then loaded his SKS, stepped on the cardboard and shot straight down at it several times. Ha ha, right?

Mr. Numbers failed to calculate for the amount of shale in the soil.

I have to say in retrospect that it was *ironically* funny. He wasn't *badly* hurt by the copper jackets that somehow managed to ricochet and imbed in his thighs and groin, barely missing what counts. He got himself to the ER. I can only imagine what he told the docs.

This was our first and last casualty. The West Virginia Free Militia never met again.

SHOOTING UP

The second incident stands out as the single most dangerous thing I have ever seen on the firing line. Against my better judgment, I was shooting at the local public range, a place that requires considerable awareness of the shooters out there with you. I'll never forget it.

Two men were shooting at hand-thrown clay pigeons that were lofted well over the backstop into the clear blue sky. This is fine, so long as you use a shotgun. These guys were using an SKS *rifle*. I was so stunned that I actually froze, but then they did it again, only this time they spewed a burst of bullets.

I had a quick decision to make. I had to confront these idiots. I'll be politically correct and say that they didn't look like West Virginia locals—a fact confirmed when I said, "Hey! Do you have an idea where those bullets are going land? Don't you know that Morgantown is on the other side of the ridge?"

Either they didn't know, didn't speak English, or didn't care. They just sneered and did it again! Other people at the range took notice of this breathtakingly stupid duo. A couple of them joined me in insisting that they stop firing.

"Hey, man! Could you please put down that gun for a minute? You are not being safe."

The look of fury in the gunner's eyes gave us all pause. He reloaded. For a second I thought he was going to turn on us. Everybody reached for a weapon…

That was a very, very tense moment. The unspoken challenge just hung in the air, like some sort of showdown. The idiot turned and fired a ten-shot burst into the closest backstop. He and his buddy then sped off in their truck. One of the other shooters got the license number and called the cops.

These are just the kind of shooters who should be banned from ever owning any sort of gun. They give us all a bad name. So far as I know, their bullets didn't make the news, thank goodness.

THE PROTOTYPE

Finland, 1940

Finnish ski troops of the twenty-eighth infantry regiment glided silently through the forest with their sledded Lahti 20 mm cannon in tow. Their objective was an isolated pocket of Soviet troops that had formed a defensive circle and killed their horses for food. There were dozens of these desperate "mottos" on the shores of Lake Ladoga, but there were far too few of Finland's pride to conduct any sort of siege. All hopes were pinned on a rapid series of hit-and-run attacks designed to leave the impression that the ghostly Finns were everywhere. If the Soviets ever realized how few men opposed them and how lightly they were armed, all would be lost.

Simo and his three men left their skis in the covert of the trees to complete their approach to the target on foot. Their whiteouts were perfect, and they knew the ground. A Russian eye was never made that could see them. With luck, the enemy's tanks would be destroyed or captured within the hour.

Sporadic rifle and machinegun fire broke out on the other side of the target. Mortars laid a smoke screen for an attack that would not come. The Soviets fell for the ruse and concentrated their forces in the wrong direction.

"There's our cover," Simo said with a smile. "Not far now."

✛ ✛ ✛

Petrov, Vacovi, and Simonov commanded the three tanks that were trapped in the pocket. Their engines idled as they waited for orders. Vacovi's tank had trouble with the right track. His driver and gunner were attempting to mend it. The brief flurry of small arms and smoke motivated the surviving officers to rethink their defenses.

"Another quick attack," Petrov said.

"I don't think there are that many of them out there. They're just trying to keep us awake. Let's get Uri and go the command post."

Uri Simonov's T-26 light tank was a copy of a British design that had once been a world beater. For a few years during the Spanish Civil War, it outshined anything the Germans or Italians could field. Russian T-26 tanks also fought with distinction against the Japanese, though the armor was thought to be too light, and it was brought up to 25 mm on later models. The type's sloppy welding often left openings in the superstructure that let in both Molotov cocktail flames and flooding water. While Uri was always concerned about his tank's thin armor and slow speed, its powerful 45 mm gun could fire high explosive and antitank rounds. There was also a .30-caliber machinegun mounted beside the main gun with more than three thousand rounds ready to go. He had superior firepower, but he also had problems seeing his targets when buttoned up in the cramped turret.

Uri's original formation came to Finland with twenty-four tanks of all types. Fuel starvation and mechanical breakdowns in the minus twenty-five-degree temperatures doomed half of his comrades' tanks before they could fire a single shot. Then the Finns had their say with flame and improvised explosives—weapons that required near suicidal courage to use. They cut the roads and captured many Russian weapons in raids on their supply lines. Only officers were taken prisoner. Those who didn't die in an ambush were left to freeze.

Petrov and Vacovi banged on their comrade's turret.

"Uri! There's a meeting for the tank commanders; let's go."

A voice echoed from within, "I can't find my map case."

"I'll bet he's got a bottle of vodka in there." Vacovi climbed up on the track and looked in the open hatches. "What do you care about a map case?" he muttered. "We aren't going anywhere. Hey! Don't play with that in this cold!" He made a rude gesture. Petrov wasn't in the mood for jokes.

"To hell with you, Vacovi!" Uri raged.

"Let's go, children," Petrov scolded. "The commissar is watching."

✛ ✛ ✛

Simo was arguably the most respected marksman in Finland, and from the very outset of the Winter War, he used his skills to make some legendary shots. He was specifically requested for the L-39 antitank gun project by the weapon's designer, the famous Aimo Lahti, himself. They worked well together, particularly on the stock, offset sights, and the horrible trigger.

Over the course of the weapon's development, Simo, Aimo, and factory technicians fired thousands of rounds from point blank range to more than a thousand yards. Targets included steel plates that varied in thickness from 10 mm to 25 mm. The armor piecing ammunition could penetrate 15 mm of hardened plate at five hundred yards, though at showdown ranges performance was somewhat better. The design team had no way of knowing that the British made steel they used for targets was of a much higher quality than most Russian armor that in some cases could be penetrated by mere rifle bullets.

The Solothurn Rheinmetal-Borsig made rounds measured 20 mm by 138 mm and weighed over a pound. Simo could load the weapon with high explosive rounds as well as, armor piercing with penetrator, antitank tracer, and a rather dangerous to handle incendiary round.

THE L-39 HAS A SET OF SMALL SKIS THAT WERE MEANT TO BE USED WHEN GETTING THE WEAPON INTO POSITION. AS CAN BE SEEN, THERE IS A BIPOD WITH A HYDRAULIC BUFFER FOLDED IN FRONT OF THE SKIS FROM WHICH THE SMART GUNNER WILL FIRE THE RIFLE. THE FINNS REFERRED TO THE LAHTI DESIGN AS AN "ELEPHANT GUN." BY 1940 IT WAS ALL BUT USELESS IN ITS INTENDED ROLL. NOTE THE OFFSET SIGHTS, CHEEK REST, AND RECOIL PAD.

For the L-39, armor penetration was the issue, but weapon recoil was the problem. The elephant gun's ferocious kick was dampened by the semiautomatic action, a muzzle brake, and sheer weight. The trio's combined effectiveness was not truly appreciated until the first time the rifle failed to eject a shell. The malfunction translated into twenty-five percent more recoil, as Simo learned too well. He insisted that he was none the worse for wear, though every one of his teeth was loose.

Simo advised the technicians, "If you grab onto it for dear life and shoot it using the bipod, you can stand the recoil. But God help you if you shoot it on just its skis. The average soldier can't fire this thing without a lot of training."

The Finns' stunning successes against Stalin's massive armies took an ever greater toll on their limited resources. The Soviets solved their earlier logistical problems and rid themselves of incompetent officers. The Finns were thrown back, and the enemy advanced all along the frontier. In one sector the Finns were completely routed and dropped all their supplies to escape the Soviet pincers. The enemy lost all momentum, however, when they over ran enemy field kitchens that were brimming with sausages. The Finns were literally saved by pork.

With their backs to the proverbial frozen wall, Finland's high command sent everyone and everything capable of battle to the front. This included Simo and the L-39 prototype.

Simo selected a three-man team to be his ammunition bearers, spotters, and to act as security for the gun in the field. They carried Soumi automatic carbines with seventy round drum magazines. They practiced disassembly and maintenance of the L-39, loading different types of ammunition, and packing the weapon for snow travel. Finally, each man fired the elephant gun and swore that he would take up the rifle to carry on the fight.

They went straight into action. Much to the amazement of his comrades, Simo stopped a light tank at more than four hundred meters.

Over the following days, news of Simo's elephant gun travelled the trenches. He used the rifle on targets he had never considered possible without a field gun. He fired incendiary and explosive rounds into the embrasures of Soviet fortifications. It was employed against snipers, and there was talk of using the volatile incendiary round in the dry season to kill trapped Russians in forest fires.

The L-39 had its limitations. Simo shot it out with a BT-7 light tank at less than one hundred yards. The tank's 22 mm of sloped frontal armor withstood repeated hits. He might have been crushed under its tracks, but the tank had to climb over an obstacle. Its nose began to rise, and before it could tip back down, Simo rapid fired armor piercing shells into the beast's thin underbelly. It caught fire and burned all night.

+ + +

The silent gun team slid through the labyrinth of fallen, snow-covered trees. The wind picked up, blowing snow that added to their cover. The distracting smoke screen, however, wafted away without an assault, and Finn rifle fire from the tree line was desultory at best. Even the dreaded Finnish mortars were silent.

The Soviet officers cursed themselves for their cowardice and prayed that their commanders never got wind of their mistake. There wasn't an officer on the line who hadn't pictured himself in front of a firing squad. The only way to prove one's loyalty to Comrade Stalin was to pay whatever the cost in lives to achieve some sort of victory.

Simo slithered from cover to cover until he found the perfect side on view of the tanks. They were close, barely two hundred yards away. "Here, quietly," Simo whispered. "We want the bipod on this log down here, and we'll have the cover of these trees on the flanks."

The L-39 was painted white. Amid the branches and shrubs, it was invisible. Three magazines waited by the gun, each with a different type of shell. Simo prepared to load the weapon, but two Russian soldiers with shovel and pick began to dig a foxhole a bare thirty yards in front of Simo's hide. Other Soviets carried ammunition boxes and a heavy machinegun up from the road.

"Bad luck for us, Simo. If you cock the rifle now, they will hear."

"I will handle the gun alone. You three spread out. Keep them off me for a minute. That's all I need."

✦ ✦ ✦

The Russians digging in were hungry and cold. Their diet of black bread, horsemeat, and tea was not sufficient to keep them operating at anywhere near an acceptable level of proficiency. Only fear of the commissars' pistol kept them moving, but even so, it was at an understandable glacial speed.

Both of the diggers heard a tremendous mechanical *clack!* They knew that they were in trouble, but the feeling only lasted for a few fleeting seconds.

Three Soumi carbines fired short bursts that took their enemies by surprise as Simo set to work.

Uri was tucked in the turret of his tank, talking to his new gunner and looking for the flask in his map case when Simo's first shot struck the turret's side vision port. The armor-piercing shell punched through and broke into a shower of white-hot shards and steel spall. His gunner was killed instantly when a bite-sized chunk of metal clipped his neck. Uri was cut severely on his scalp, neck, and shoulders. He yelled, "Driver! turn left!"

It was his last command, and an empty one. Simo hit the vision port again.

Petrov and Vacovi dashed back to their mounts and climbed up the right side to avoid incoming automatic fire. The tank commanders felt Simo's 20 mm cannon rounds hit and penetrate their turrets, and they knew that anyone in the tank was surely dead. Vacovi was relieved to see his gunner lying in a ditch very much alive.

✛ ✛ ✛

Simo counted his shots as he centered his crude slight on each tank's turret. They were so close that 20 mm of buttery steel just wasn't enough to stop an armor-piercing shell. He debated firing additional rounds at the tanks. He hoped to kill the crew and leave them as salvageable prizes for his tank-starved army. He rocked the second magazine in place and used his field glasses to see if the tanks were still active. The heat radiating from the fifty inch jacketed barrel blurred his view, but he could see well enough to pick out an officer rallying a platoon of infantry. He could also see the middle T-26 turret rotating in his direction.

✛ ✛ ✛

Petrov managed to slide into his seat at the back of the turret without being hit, but his gunner was missing. He also noticed two holes in the turret at shoulder level. If the missing crewman had been at his post, his headless remains would have blocked Petrov from taking over the weapon's controls. He moved into the gunner's seat and traversed the main gun to the left as he looked through his optic for Simo's elephant gun.

If the L-39 had a vice, it was the necessary muzzle brake that doubled an already vicious report and blasted a horizontal flame several feet to each side. Petrov had crossed swords with the dreaded antitank weapons before, and he knew exactly what to look for.

"There he is!" Petrov growled into his communication tube. No response. He stabbed his driver signal button, "Driver! Advance! Come left!" The tank did not move. The commander could not see the third crewman wither as he bled out in his seat.

Petrov traversed the turret, but Simo fired first. His round hit just below the turret where the armor was not sufficiently sloped to keep the Lahti's high-explosive shells from igniting the stored ammunition. The explosion ripped the turret off its ring.

✛ ✛ ✛

Simo's snap decision to destroy the active tank did nothing to stop the infantry charging toward him. There was no time to pick up another weapon. He fired at the officer and flipped him in the air. The platoon's bayonet charge ended in another hail-of-burp gun fire. The support team anticipated a second counterattack, and they knew from experience that the enemy would come on in veritable overwhelming numbers.

"Simo! Let's get the gun out of here!"

"Wait," Simo called. "The third tank is moving!"

✛ ✛ ✛

Vacovi and his gunner had reoccupied their tank and prepared to fire the main gun. The cannon fired and the case ejected, but he missed his shot by less than a foot. Simo could feel the pressure of the shell's wake. He yelled to his men, "Get out any way you can!" Then he turned to his gun and loaded a fresh magazine. He pulled the massive bolt-release trigger, but it only partially closed. He could feel a malfunction.

Simo reached to the right of the gun to crank the rack and pinion cocking lever. He rotated it one-and-a-half times, and the bolt latch click told him the breach was open. A bullet streaked over the rifle, missing the magazine by millimeters only to hit Simo in the collarbone. For a few seconds, he was dazed, and he lost concentration. He pushed the magazine release with his left hand and then rocked the magazine forward. The offending round fell free. Another Russian bullet hit Simo's helmet and grazed his scalp. Again he lost track of his objective. His vision returned, and he could see a dozen riflemen charging toward him. The clip fell back into place, and he pulled the heavy stock tight to his bleeding shoulder. He squeezed the bolt release, and this time he could feel it close correctly. The sights settled on the third tank, and he fired five rounds in rapid succession. The deafening blast covered his cries of agony as he felt the bone break.

HERE WE CAN SEE THE L-39'S COCKING HANDLE. IT MUST BE ROTATED ONE-AND-A-HALF TIMES TO LOCK IN THE OPEN POSITION. THE LEVER BELOW THE TRIGGER LOOKS LIKE A GRIP SAFETY. IT IS ACTUALLY THE BOLT RELEASE. AFTER COCKING, GREAT CARE MUST BE TAKEN TO ROTATE THE LEVER FORWARD UNTIL IT CLICKS OR IT WILL SPIN AND BREAK YOUR FINGERS.

✛ ✛ ✛

Simo was killed by the most primitive weapon on the battlefield when a spike bayonet finished him. The Finns mounted a counterattack and gave many more lives to retrieve their elephant gun. Lahti's prototype was sent back to the factory for inspection. Its designer was deeply saddened to have lost Simo.

Aimo tore the gun to pieces to examine each part for wear. There were no mechanical issues. The L-39 was ready for mass production. After the war, surviving L-39 cannons went through arsenal rebuilds where damaged guns were broken down and their parts used as spares for other weapons. The surviving guns went into storage for fifteen dark years.

Then, in 1958, one thousand L-39s were sold off on the world market along with two hundred thousand armor-piercing rounds. One hundred of these heavy weapons were imported by Interarmco and sold in Virginia by Potomac Arms. One of these was purchased by a college student who had no way of knowing what his new toy had been through or that the trigger itself was scavenged from Aimo and Simo's original Lahti L-39 prototype.

CHAPTER 3

Toys

THE HEAVY HITTERS

Meadow Lane Farm, 1959

THIS LAHTI ANTITANK GUN MADE SHORT WORK OF A COMPACT CAR. IT IS
BEING FIRED AT A MACHINEGUN SHOOT IN WEST VIRGINIA, 2010.

When my father was a young man, he had piles of money. His
great-grandfather invented the concrete interlocking pipe, which
revolutionized city engineering and farm irrigation. Lock Joint Pipe did
major infrastructure work at the Kennedy Space Center, and during
World War II, the company built the water system for the Manhattan
Project which gave the United States its first atomic bomb.

So we are a family of plumbers who have always loved guns. We had
plenty of space to shoot them on our property in Bath County, Virginia.

112

Dad had just about every kind of rifle, shotgun, and pistol one could imagine, but he had no cannon. And cannons are, quite obviously to us, the ultimate toys.

The Potomac Arms Company was located near the old torpedo factory in Alexandria, Virginia. The shop sold surplus weapons by the hundred and just so happened to have a Lahti, L-39 in pristine condition for the low, low price of one hundred dollars. It came in its own seven-foot-long wooden crate with all the accessories, two magazines, and fifty armor-piercing rounds. The price reflected in 2014 dollars computes to a little over eight hundred bucks. The shells sold individually for .89 cents each. Today, if you can find them, they sell for eighty dollars to one hundred dollars a pop. The gun itself will cost you at least fifteen grand. Because the rifle has a bore over one-half inch, The Bureau of Alcohol, Tobacco and Firearms classifies the beast as a *destructive device* and thus it has to be registered with the federal government in the same manner as a machinegun. In 1960, however, the L-39 was sold just like any other rifle.

"I just had to have it," Dad said. "I was so excited about it that I drove my Mercedes convertible to the farm, got the truck, and drove back to the store that day. It was ten hours, round trip. We took it to the pond area where there was an old telephone pole that was no longer in use. We set up on the overlook. I'd say it was a one hundred yard shot. I fired and drilled a perfect 20 mm hole right through it. Two more rounds cut it in half."

Over the next few years, Dad and Kyle fired the L-39 at motor blocks, boulders, groundhogs, deer, and their favorite target of all, beaver dams. The rifle was not perfect for farm use. The blast was loud enough to be heard in the next county, and the rounds tended to ricochet if great care was not taken to hit the target square on.

It is a little known fact that people who have cannons like to show them off. The Hirsh gang sat the rifle on two hay bales in the back of their old pick-up. They drove it all around the county in some sort of a victory lap that today I find unimaginable. They wound up by slowly rolling around the Homestead Resort's front drive. The doormen didn't know whether to laugh or run. Dad had even added a couple German helmets hanging to add to the effect.

Nobody made a sound. Ten seconds passed, and they drove on. Minutes later the sheriff pulled them over. He walked up to the familiar truck.

"Oh, you two. I thought I was going to have to put the wood to somebody." He put away his night stick. "Don't drive that damn thing around, you hear? I'd hate to hear your father if he found out." He stared the college boys down. "How does it shoot?"

Pretty soon everyone in Bath County knew that the Hirsh family was the most heavily armed bunch of Episcopalians for hundreds, if not thousands, of miles in any direction.

This was a footnote that my grandfather didn't want in his autobiography.

I never saw the antitank gun fired. I have early childhood memories of it because it was stored in the machinery barn where I liked to play. There was a serious dispute about the gun between Dad and my antigun grandfather, a man whose insensitivity and pompousness were unmatched on this side of the Atlantic Ocean. He decided that my father just shouldn't have the weapon and gave it away to a literal stranger who happened to be at the farm appraising some antiques.

Pop had no idea that by that point in time, the gun was registered with BATF. You cannot just hand it off to piss off your kid. This created a supreme paperwork nightmare that took years to amicably resolve with the government. The forms are in the Hirsh family files.

✦ ✦ ✦

It would be more than thirty years before I found another L-39 Lahti in my gun guru's shop in Morgantown, West Virginia. His has been converted to fire .50-caliber bullets, and so it is classified as a standard rifle, not a Destructive Device that has to be registered. My father commented that his full-bore 20 mm cannon hit you twice with each shot. The first slam came from the recoil of the detonated round, and the second part was the hit from the massive bolt slamming into the rear of the receiver. I would love to have known that pain. The .50-caliber version has all the recoil of a BB gun.

A few days ago, I took the converted Lahti L-39 on an expedition with my son, his pals and a best friend who has a Barrett .50-caliber rifle to White Horse Range in Barbour County, West Virginia. Safety was on my mind as I do have one major concern about shooting these heavy rifles. I have found that .50 rounds like to ricochet. In fact, there is a YouTube video of a man who shoots a Barrett .50-caliber rifle at a steel plate, only to have the round bounce back and rip his headphones off! White Horse is one of the safest ranges I have ever used, and there was no chance of a round bouncing off to points unknown.

The Barrett has a huge muzzle brake that blasts a massive amount of expanding gas at a forty-five-degree angle back toward the bystanders who always gather to watch when a .50 caliber is in play. The Barrett was extremely accurate. Groups fired came in at less than one inch. We did not fire the Lahti for accuracy. The offset open sights are nearly useless for precision work. They are quite adequate for their intended use against enemy armor.

There are those who say that .50-caliber rifles should be banned as they can be used to shoot down aircraft and take out armored trucks, which is their intended military use. They have been banned in California, so a new, slightly less powerful round was developed to take the .50's place. These heavy-hitter rifles represent the extreme edge of what a civilian may own without special licensure. I expect that they will be banned nationally at some point in the not too distant future, and those who have them will no doubt have to register them.

Fifty caliber ammunition is very expensive. Our little range session cost us about seventy-five dollars for the twenty rounds we fired. It is possible to reload the empties, but a special press is needed and the components are very expensive to ship. Stockpiling ammo is an expensive must-do as I can see an anti-gun strategy of allowing the rifles but banning the ammunition. Run-of-the-mill, full-metal-jacket ammunition will cost you five bucks a round—when you can find it.

SHOOTING A MODERN .50-CALIBER RIFLE IS AS CLOSE AS WE CAN GET TO THE LAHTI. IT IS A PIPSQUEAK IN COMPARISON.

This story has been a long time in the making. It began in 1939 when the first of these monster rifles was produced. There can be no question that the weapon in these pictures was used against the Russians. The story was put on pause until the late 1950s when the antitank rifle was imported and my dad got a hold of it. It was used thereafter for the sheer joy of shooting it (big joy). Then the family antitank gun slipped away, and a malaise fell on us. We had no cannon. It was hard to live with the shame of it all.

But we did recover. The advent of the Barrett .50-caliber rifle gave us a glimmer of hope that a cannon, albeit a small one, could once again be ours. Then serendipity fell from the stars, and a Lahti L-39 materialized before us. Yes, it fired a puny bullet, but the rest was as it should be. I got to cock it, let the bolt fly home, and squeeze the trigger.

The borrowed Lahti spent the night before these pictures were taken in my living room, sitting on a wooden crate. My son's friends passed through. They usually ignore us, but this time they stopped for pictures. "Oh my God! My dad has to see this!"

"Do I want your dad to see this?" I asked.

"Oh, yeah. He's from South Africa."

My wife came through the door and didn't miss a beat. "So that's it, huh? It kinda dominates the room. How long will it be here? Not that I don't like it. It is oddly interesting. I wish you could see yourself. Your smile is blinding."

I couldn't hide it. I said, "You know, I gotta tell you—just having the antitank gun in the house makes me feel a whole ten percent better about life."

"You are going to have to give it back," she chided.

"Don't worry. As soon as I sell my gun book, I'll get one."

"I'm not worried," she said as she gave me a hug. "Just make sure you also buy me a living room large enough to hold it."

And so ends the Lahti saga: Once upon a time, it was the largest shoulder weapon an American shooter could buy. Now it has been neutered, which is both a sign of the times and the last stand of the antitank gun.

Red Rider:

Lexington, VA, 1994

I t was Christmas 1993. My wife, three year old son, and I were with my father and his wife, Sue. My two much younger half sisters, Lindsley and Caroline, were among our throng. My stepbrother and stepsister had their respective significant others along. We were all very festive, especially Kristin, whose beau was meeting the family for the first time.

Pavel was at that time an up-and-coming photographer in New York. He was originally from Prague in the Czech Republic, and he had a serious accent. He spoke passionately about his career and Kristin. I pictured him at some art show, glass of wine in hand, discussing light and shadow. He was a little reserved at first, but Pavel was warm and interesting. Nobody quite knew what to make of him other than to say, "Kristin is lucky. I like that guy."

It was seventy-two degrees in Virginia that Christmas morn. The grass was green. The sky was a deep blue. It was a little weird. Christmas with a three-year-old is always fun, but I want to jump ahead to the part about me—and the gift that made the day memorable.

My wife gave me a carbon-dioxide-powered BB rifle. It could also shoot .177 air pellets. I was very pleased, and my son who picked it out from three options at Wal-Mart beamed at me. Then things began to spin. Pavel asked to see it, and he grabbed the box to actually read the instructions.

My stepbrother said, "Hey, wait a minute…" My dad jumped up too.

They climbed up into the attic and came down with a Crossman air gun and an original Red Rider, lever-action BB gun, just like Ralphie wanted in the famous movie, *A Christmas Story*.

The split-rail fence in the backyard borders twenty acres of woods. We could pot away without worry. And we did for hours. People came and went, trading off to go inside for other activities. New shooters need targets that move to add excitement to the experience so we shot what are known as "reactive targets" rather than paper bull's-eyes. Occasionally one of us would come up with something extra shootable, and everyone wanted a turn. We zapped the ugly Christmas tree bulbs early on. We hung targets from trees, shot them in the air, and we played a version of H-O-R-S-E with BBs substituted for a basketball. We also played "Step Back," a game designed to get you the optimum distance for your skill level and the capability of the gun. BBs are obviously round and unspun as they leave the muzzle. So after about ten yards, they fly wild, and hitting becomes a matter of luck.

Forrest shot for the first time. Dad and Sue's friends popped by, and we got them out there. We shot thousands of BBs and hundreds of pellets. We learned something about Pavel, too. He was a European who knew how to shoot.

On that day, the cheap BB gun was the best caliber for an audience of inexperienced shooters. They needed no earplugs, and they could try,

try, try, until they hit their targets. It took about two minutes for people to figure out the proper sight picture. Christmas was never better, but my new BB rifle gave up the ghost that very day. Apparently the life span of the Wal-Mart air rifle is a lot shorter than it used to be, but the Red Rider shot on as it has for fifty years.

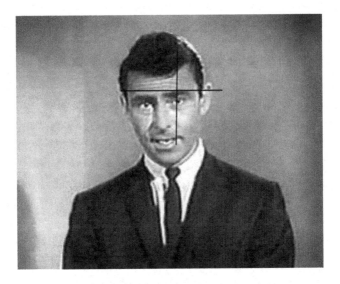

CHRISTMAS WITH ROD:

Washington, DC, 1974

I was twelve, and as far as Christmases go, I'd had a very good day. My new stepfather was trying to make a point. I was given electric trains out the wazoo, a stereo with a high-end turntable, records, and a new bike with gears. The biggy was pure ecstasy. Santa brought me the Holy Grail of gifts—a Buck Knife—the Folding Hunter with four inch blade. Finally, I had a proper weapon to hang on my belt when Mom wasn't around.

We attended the stepfamily's Christmas party thrown by my new Uncle Walter. They had a gorgeous house in northwest Washington, DC. When we arrived, there were already twenty expensive cars in his driveway, and inside there was a "rocks" glass in every hand. My folks like their eggnog with extra whatever that undrinkable beverage has in it. Failing that, anything else you have at the bar will serve. I remember looking around the room at the score or more of guests who certainly were gay and Christmas elegant. Red and green dresses. The men in suits. Even I had been thrust into my finest blue blazer.

I had about ten Cokes and a mountain of Swiss chocolate. Food was everywhere. Caviar, smoked salmon, shrimp, or roast beef—go for it. Soon I was swept up in the exuberance. There were no tedious Christmas songs a'playing. A very acceptable mix of Sinatra, Elvis, and Ray Charles took the stage. The tree was massive and blinking away. Wrapping paper was everywhere. Champagne flowed. I was given a glass, which became two or more. The beer course was served, but my mom cut me off. There was snow on the ground, and I had a huge knife in my pocket. Like I said, all was right that Christmas night.

Then I discovered my new cousin's big gift, a Crossman air rifle.

I had retreated to the TV room where Tom was already hovering, waiting for his buds to show up and free him from the nightmare of spending time with his parents. He was friendly and showed me the rifle. He explained that it was in essence a bolt action. "Open here. See the BB? Close, pump, aim, fire."

His friends swooped in. Tom handed me the gun and was gone into the night. I opened the bolt, looked inside the breech, and saw no BB. I closed the bolt and pumped it up three times. I sat in the big easy chair about five feet from the big TV screen. It was eleven o'clock; WTTG Channel Five was still on the air. I had Rod Serling in the scope's crosshairs as he famously announced, "The next stop...the *Twilight Zone.*"

And that's when I shot him.

I can still hear the rifle spit and the pellet *tink!* The picture immediately shrank to a six-inch band across the middle of the screen. I could still see the program going on right beneath the point of impact.

We all know that sinking feeling. First, it's, "No! That didn't just happen!" Then it's followed by the horrible, "Yes...it did..." And the new reality sets in. We mutter some version of, "I am so screwed." I was utterly baffled. I remember yelling at myself, "How the hell did a BB get in there?" I never found out.

So I sucked it up and thought, *Just get it over with.* I marched straight out and somberly announced to all, "Hey, I just shot the TV with Tom's air rifle. Sorry."

Uncle Wally looked shocked and let out the best, most welcome laugh I have ever heard. He rocked back and whooped like I scored a winning touchdown in overtime. That laughter spread rapidly across the room. Their joyous noise swelled, and some were wiping tears from their eyes. My mother stopped laughing, but she just couldn't sustain the straight face needed to project shame and guilt for the offense. They just waved me off. Take a pass. It was like they were all in the Mob and telling me, "Forgetaboutit."

And that was that. I didn't even want to touch a gun for a long time thereafter. I was really shaken by the experience. Sadly, my gun safety didn't really improve. There would be other close calls.

So I have this Christmas memory like clockwork every year. And as family tradition would have it, we always watch *A Christmas Story* and Ralphie's BB gun quest. Seriously, that kid should have had my problem. I didn't shoot my eye out, but old Rod lost one of his.

THE FARMER MAFIA

Meadow Lane, 1995

P est control—our farm manager told me that there were too many
pigeons in the barn. "Your grandmother (his boss) won't let me do
anything about it! You know how she gets about her animals. You can't
walk down them stalls without being bombed by pigeon shit! You can't
park the truck in there." He went on and on. They were eating the
bird feed, and they had about a thousand nests in the hayloft. He ran
through one reason after another to despise the birds.

We were speaking in a kind of farmer's code, which is really a
trial and judgment for animals that get in the way. It's the same kind
of communication that a mob boss uses when he says, "God forbid

something might happen to Paulie." The capo gets the message: Paulie is toast.

My youngest sister, Caroline, was visiting that very same grandmother when the subject of the pigeons came up at the dinner table. She was in high school—maybe tenth grade. "Oh, the pigeons are so beautiful! I love them, too," she cooed. I nearly barfed.

As usual, my grandma had one too many red wines, and she was off to sleep before dark. Caroline and I loaded up the BB guns and made the hit.

Back in the late twenties, my great grandmother raised unsuccessful racehorses. The horse barn is about fifty yards long with a dozen stalls on each side and an open driveway that runs down the middle. Ground to rooftop rafters is about twenty-five feet. Strategy wise, it's a bad idea to stand below the pigeon and shoot straight up at it. We had to tie a rope to the guns, climb a scary thin ladder to get into the hayloft, and then pull up the weapons. We turned on the lights and went to work.

Even after dark, a barn full of animals is a noisy place. The nearly silent weapons didn't startle the birds. It was the Saint Valentine's Day Massacre all over again.

Caroline, it turns out, has a killer instinct. She was having almost as much fun as my Springer spaniel who lunged on every bird as it fell from the rafters. There were feathers everywhere.

"You have no idea," Caroline said, "because you don't live in a city, how many times I have wanted to do this." She gave the Red Rider an ammo-checking shake, looked me right in the eye, and said with a smile, "You're never too busy to hate a pigeon."

The shooting went on for about an hour. It was all Caroline and the dog. I have never seen this side of my sister since. But I know it's there. We had to sanitize the crime scene, which was a rather time-consuming process. We filled two large grain sacks with mangled birds.

Caroline was very efficient and announced, "OK, I think we were never here. Let's go dump the evidence. What are we going to do about the dog? Jesus, look at that face. She's all dried blood and feathers. Look at that tail go!"

Dog lovers will die defending their favorite breed and know every unique quality that sets their poufy doodle above all others. I am a spaniel lover. You can run these guys through the worst bogs imaginable, and dirt doesn't cling to them. It simply falls away. We tossed a stick in the pond, and Julie went after it with her usual determination. She came out dog-show clean.

It took my grandmother a proverbial ten seconds to notice that the pigeons had disappeared. "What do you suppose could have happened?" she asked. She was very concerned. I played dumb. The farm manager gave her the farmer mafia version of, "Paulie is in the witness protection program." The cover-up didn't seem to take, and my grandma was deeply suspicious about the whole thing.

She told me, "The manager said that a bunch of red-tailed hawks came to the area and killed the pigeons. I don't buy it. Where are all the feathers? They went without a struggle? It's all very strange."

I said that I had to be going home, and I tried to disengage, but she got a hold of my arm and declared, "No, you stay. Let's drive up to the barns. I need your help with a little justice problem."

I swallowed hard as she handed me her car keys. I was about to be disinherited. She rambled on about breaking her rules and the consequences for the offense. She was still talking as she motioned for me to back up to the chicken pens.

"Leave it running," she said. She opened the trunk and pulled out a large pillowcase.

My grandmother was in her early eighties but still quite lithe. She loved the finer things, but she was at her best stalking lions on the African plains or milking Buttercup in the dairy. She ruled the barns and knew every animal in it by species and pet name. Even without the pigeons, we had birds by the hundred. They were mostly exotic chickens, but we also raised ducks, geese, and peacock.

She handed me the pillowcase. "Here. Hold this open."

She waded out into the flock, cluck clucking in her own bizarre way, and grabbed Charlie, the biggest, baddest rooster of them all.

Charlie the Rooster had been around the neighborhood for a very long time and everyone in the barnyard paid him proper respect. He was a proverbial made man, and so he fearlessly chased everyone, including cats and dogs. But one fine day he went too far and viciously pecked my grandmother's guest. The verdict was swift. My grandma scooped him up, and in one fluid motion she folded his wings against his breast and slid him headfirst in the bag.

"Hand it to me. I'll take that from here." Charlie was weirdly calm as she wrapped the open end of the pillowcase around the tailpipe of her Mercedes. "Give it some gas."

I did as I was asked and within about ten seconds it was over. She handed me the bag and told me to take it to the taxidermist. It was the single smoothest farmer mafia hit I have ever seen. She smiled over her handiwork.

"There. You see, not one ruffled feather, and it's all tied in a bow."

THE RABBIT TEST

Easton, MD, 1976

S hooting pigeons in the barn is fun, but I'd rather shoot doves in Argentina. I don't often get the chance. For me, the next best thing is rabbit hunting. They are tasty, and jumping them up from the hedgerow and popping them with the .410 was a treasured way to spend a late fall afternoon.

By the time I was twelve, I had a light recurve bow and was free to use it as I saw fit. I went after the rabbits, but I was forever losing arrows. Dad took pity on me and bought me a Benjamin air rifle. It took every bit of strength I had to pump it up eight times for maximum power. It shot perfectly formed 5 mm pellets from a rifled barrel.

I had a good 4 power scope on it, and I found that I could hit a rabbit in the head at twenty-five yards with total dependability. Dad helped me zero it. We shot it in exactly the same fashion as the .22 matches at summer camp. We also talked about hunting strategies.

Dad wanted me to be successful, and he pointed out that the bunnies appeared in the soybean fields just before dusk. I learned that I had to freeze and shoot from wherever I was when I first saw the target. I often had to shoot offhand, which is the toughest position by far. When I missed, generally I could see the dirt kick up a little dust. I discovered "Kentucky Windage," and pretty soon I had a pile of rabbits skinned, cleaned, and ready for the freezer.

Prior to this, I had done a great deal of formal target shooting at camp, but most of it was done from the prone position at twenty-five yards. Under those conditions I didn't need to know anything about trajectories and velocity. I didn't have to factor for wind. Air pellets run out of steam quickly, and they are blown off course by the slightest breeze. That Benjamin air rifle taught me the basics of using a rifle in the field. As such, it is one of the most important shooting irons I have ever owned.

OPERATION ANNIHILATE:

On the Road, 1974

I can't remember exactly when it was, but when I was very young my father bought a BB gun from the back of *Boy's Life Magazine* called the **Annihilator**. It looked like a space gun with a plastic, ventilated barrel. It had no sights at all. It didn't need them because this weapon fired one way—full auto.

The **Annihilator** receiver was basically a giant BB reservoir. It held thousands of the things, so many in fact that you had to pour graphite in there to get the feeding right. It was powered by cans of Freon that apparently people could buy at Western Auto, our sole source in Bath County for everything. The store manager was very interested in the gun, and I recall how he puzzled with dad over how to attach the ozone-layer-killing can under the weapon. They figured it out, but they had to improvise a better gasket. With the **Annihilator** charged up and ready for action it seemed logical to us that we should shoot it out of the car window as we whizzed back to the farm. Remember that this all took place in the boondocks of Appalachia. Our reasoning was just a little different. It's a context issue.

We blasted away at crows eating a dead groundhog on the roadside. We tried to shoot a few road signs, but much to our disappointment, we found that after a squirt or two the can of Freon got too cold and lost its energy. Our neighbor's lawn ornaments were very tempting, but we had no power when the moment came for some real action. Then we had a mishap...

We were just about to turn in our lane when the Freon can came loose, and it spouted a furious fountain of white gas everywhere. Within a second Dad couldn't see the road. It was like a smoke grenade going off in the front seat.

"Get rid of it! Get rid of it!" Dad yelled. I scooped it up and tossed it out the window.

I have always wondered what the people in the car behind us thought when that smoking bomb of a grenade bounced off the road in front of them. They swerved wildly to avoid it as we made our turn.

No more was heard from the **Annihilator** for many years until one day when I was cleaning out the garage. I found it right where Dad had stashed it a couple of decades before. My five-year-old son, Hunter, and I hooked it up to an air compressor. I pointed him in a safe direction and let him blast away. I recall noticing that he was definitely left-handed, and I made a mental note that he would need a left-handed guitar. But more than that, he was laughing and smiling. We were in on something good. It was a full-automatic bonding experience made possible by something called the **Annihilator.**

Once again, the smallest projectile possible yielded the biggest fun.

CHAPTER 4

Hunting

COLD FEET

Chesapeake Bay, Modern Day

"Who's the aging preppie standing out there in the driveway? Is he on our list? He's been out there for a while now."

"You and your lists! I think he's here to pick up his son-in-law, the guy in blind number two. I heard a shot. He may be coming in soon. You really don't know who that is?"

The broad oak door swung open, and the mysterious gentleman stepped into the foyer. He paused to look at something in the dining room, then turned toward the bar with a smile.

"Hello. Hello, good morning," he said cheerfully as he extended his hand. "I see by your name tags that I am talking with…Don and… Frank. I'm John. Nice shirts."

"Thanks, we're proud to wear the name. Can we get you a cup of coffee while you wait?"

"Certainly. Just black, but only if it's no trouble."

The man with the clipboard asked, "Are you a hunter, sir? Ducks or geese perhaps?"

John smiled and said, "You *hunt* deer, but you *shoot* ducks. Both styles can be damned cold. I have done my share of shooting, especially when I was young about a million years ago. Being here brings it all back. There's something inviting about a duck blind on a frigid November morning. Ours was a quick slap-together bit of carpentry with a bench for four men, and there was a kinda half-collapsed roof over it. Rusty nails everywhere."

"We take great pride in our blinds," countered the clipboard man.

John looked confused. "No rusty nails? You call that progress? Back in those days, we had lead shot number twos that could knock a goose down at forty yards. We needed every inch because in our cove most of the birds flew right over the blind and into the fields."

The bartender nodded with a smile, "One of ours is like that."

"I shot a Browning A-5 almost exclusively. That hump-back, squared-off receiver just shouldered perfectly for me. Best fitting gun ever. Short recoil operation, no pumping to do—just boom, boom, boom and down go the birds. Mine is a real Belgian-made gun. They make them in Japan now. I've seen them. They actually look all right, but I have a real one."

"Do you shoot often?"

"Here? No. Now I go to Canada every few years or so. It's the only place where you can shoot birds in any numbers, but you can't bring the meat back with you. It's a real dance getting your guns through customs too."

"So all this must seem pretty rinky-dink."

"You guys have made it a posh experience all right. I love what you've done with this room."

The bartender nodded. "People pay for this look. They don't know that it's all knock-off stuff. There is virtually nothing authentic in here."

"You don't have to tell me. Knew it the second I walked in."

The man with the clipboard said, "Speaking of paying guests, here comes my long-overdue morning group." He checked off several things.

Four men dressed in immaculate hunting gear breezed into the room. The man with the clipboard met them graciously. John took a seat by the bay window and watched the hunting experience unfold.

A golf cart zipped up the driveway and stopped just outside the door. A neatly uniformed hunting guide carefully put the patrons' gleaming Italian automatics in a gun rack where the golf clubs should have been. A girl with an apron on trotted up with four cute, little, white box lunches. The guide produced a whisk broom to neaten up the seats.

The host hunter came to the bar and motioned for a tiny dram. He noticed John and said, "How are you today, sir? Great day for hunting! The sky is blue; it's not too cold…should be great! You do much hunting here?"

"Today it's just my son-in-law out there."

"Never been here before? They do it up nice here. They've got good Scotch and a machine that plucks the birds! What more can you ask? Am I right?"

John raised his coffee cup in a salute. "All bases covered then. Have a good hunt, Senator." There was an edge in his voice that went unnoticed by everyone but the bar man.

"Ah, you got me. My constituents wouldn't understand this. They're a bunch of citified wimps, global warming, animal rights, and all that… shit. You picked me out pretty damn quick! Not enough camouflage?"

"Not against this background I'm afraid."

The guide appeared. "Gentlemen, we are ready to take you to the blind." The hunters were jovial as they plopped into the golf carts and sped out toward the river.

"Sorry about that," the bartender said. "Person like you…"

The clipboard man returned. "Did you know we booked *a senator* for blind number two? He's expecting results. He's going to be pissed when they go all day without a shot. I told' em to be here at six a.m.

sharp. I'll bet you can shoot all day in Canada, right? It's just all around better there."

"It would have to be, but this... this *was* better. If you want to hunt pheasant, you do it out West. This was the place for water fowl. There *was* nothing like the eastern shore of Maryland."

"Did you grow up here?"

"Close enough. I'll tell you this. I grew up with a shotgun in my hands: doves, quail, rabbit, ducks, geese, and deer all with one gun. I remember one morning quite vividly. It was probably 1965, and I was in the blind, crouched, waiting to stand and cut loose on a half-dozen geese that were over the decoys. I picked mine out. I watched as it set its wings to glide in. I kept thinking, wait...wait for it...and then it dropped its feet and back flapped its wings. For a moment it was almost stationary in the air."

"So did you shoot the bird?"

"It folded right up. There were two men out there with me that morning. They were none too happy to see that I had beaten them to the blind. They fired five shots but only managed to cripple one goose that swam out of range. It was sad. I felt it. They mate for life, you know. I can identify with that.

"One guy was an old, retired judge that made fat men look like scarecrows, and the other one was a man my father just hated. But he had helped to build the blind, and we kept the decoys in his garage. They insisted that the bird I hit was in fact downed by one of them, and I was responsible for the cripple. I just sat there and took it, but I wasn't leaving.

"Later that morning a singleton flew in at twelve o'clock high, just inside shotgun range. They emptied their guns, and the goose kept going. I stood up, swung my A-5 twelve, and brought him down.

"They were actually impressed. I will never forget what the fat judge said, 'I guess we know who got that one.' They treated me differently after that shot. They even offered me a hit from their flask. I was fourteen!"

"That was with the Browning?"

"Yes, my father's twelve. He treated that gun like shit. I remember seeing it so full of rust that the bolt would freeze, and it would jam. He always said, 'A rusty gun shoots harder.' Turns out, that's not true. It's not all his fault, of course, because you can't remove the A-5's bolt or trigger unit without tapping out pins and screws. We weren't that brave."

The bar man shook his head, "The duck blind is a pretty damp environment for a gun you can't properly clean."

"You bet. And those old paper shells had to be kept dry too. They'd swell up. Have either of you even seen a paper shell?"

They hadn't.

"That gun's action got so rusty that we decided to pour about a gallon of Hoppes cleaning solvent in there, and we just kept turning it and turning it like it was a pig roast or something. We let it sit overnight, and the next day we poured out a rather nasty black sludge. Then we hit it with an air hose. The gun worked fine, but my old man had a gunsmith strip it down and reblue it, thank God."

"Did you use any other guns?

"Not really. We had a Winchester Model 12 that was a fine gun, but neither of us really liked the pump action. It had an improved cylinder choke and was actually better for grouse and quail than ducks and geese. Guests liked it. Our A5s had Cutts compensators with changeable chokes, which was pretty slick technology back at that time. That device made them unbelievably loud, though. I definitely lost hearing from shooting next to the Cutts equipped guns."

"No ear protection?"

"Well, the people who lost hearing and noticed used ear plugs. There's something about shooting at the birds, though, that keeps the noise from being bothersome. You don't notice kick either when you are in that moment. We also had a couple side by sides and an over and under, but we always missed having that third shot in case you needed to slam a cripple before it got out of range. The rule was two sure kills and reload. The third shell was for emergencies or extreme opportunity. We were somewhat flexible on this.

"By the time I was fifteen, I was harmonized with the A5. It fit me perfectly, and I could reload it in a heartbeat. It has worked under some harsh conditions. Have you ever hunted from a pit blind out in the middle of a corn field? The worst weather I ever experienced involved my sitting in a field blind with about a foot of ice water in it. We had to wear our waders and the water was about thirty-three degrees. We had a sorta chicken-wire roof with cornstalks woven through it, and the damn thing was dripping on us. There was a really thick fog that morning and there was freezing rain off and on. There was even some hail.

"Birds were on the move everywhere. We could hear them, but we couldn't see them. The cornfields had long since been harvested, but the birds were still picking them over. Anyway, long story short, we had an entire raft of perhaps a hundreds birds land right on top of us."

"I can't imagine it." The bar man brewed a new coffee and poured the storyteller a fresh cup.

"Between the wind, rain, and the geese all honking off, we could barely hear each other. The next thing we know, a goose came gliding through the gloom with his wings set like he was a jet landing on an aircraft carrier. He landed so close that I could have reached right out and grabbed him. Then it was three more here and two more there,

there, and there. Some went over us and landed in the decoys that we set up behind the pit.

"We threw back the screen and opened up on the incoming birds. The geese already on the ground took off. But we had new birds popping through, so they got away. More came in from behind us. We were twisting and turning and swinging and reloading as fast as we could because the birds in back couldn't see or hear what was happening to the birds up front! They just kept coming. The four of us fired thirty shells in less than thirty seconds.

"Good lord! You better thank your lucky stars the game warden didn't get you!"

"Nobody gave a damn. There were hundreds of thousands, if not millions of birds back in those days. We always had a gaggle pooping all over our yard. Most people hated the geese, even wished they would go away for good. In those days you could have four birds per man in the blind and six in the freezer at home. We had twenty birds down and just like that," he said, snapping his fingers, "and the shoot was over. We were drinking coffee and laughing about it by eight thirty that morning. We were giddy...like we'd seen the mother lode. There was a colored fellah that worked for our host who plucked every single one of those birds for five bucks."

"Sounds like you had your once-in-a-lifetime moment."

"We shot like that for years, son." John caught his breath. "Then steel shot came along and took all the power out of our guns, and you couldn't make the high passing shots anymore. Too many cripples. It was inhumane, but it did keep lead out of the water. Now the Chesapeake Bay is almost dead, but it wasn't lead shot that killed it."

The man with the clipboard took a cell call. "Your son-in-law just phoned. He'll be up with his bird here directly."

"He got his bird? Good for him."

"He shot the limit. That ten gauge he's using is imposing."

"It once was. Those monster three-and-a-half-inch shells can bring a bird down out to seventy-five yards with steel or even eighty yards with lead shot. It weights about six-hundred pounds loaded, which is good because those ten gauges will hit you. It is expensive to shoot, too. I suppose if you're only allowed to shoot one goose at a time, a box of shells could last a few years. By the time that gun came along, our family was changing, moving around. We wound up in the Virginia mountains, using the ten gauge as a turkey gun."

"Do you shoot many turkeys?"

"More than you guys shoot geese. We're missing the big question, men. Where are all the birds?"

The clipboard man said, "They're getting fewer and fewer all the time. If we didn't offer skeet, trap, and sporting clays, we would be out of business. You think it has something to do with global warming?"

"I dunno. That's for the scientists. I'm just an old shooter. What do I know, right? Thanks for the coffee. I'll wait outside."

John closed the heavy door behind him and walked across the graveled drive. He looked out on the river and drifted back to a time when his feet were numb, and he couldn't feel his nose. It was a welcome pain—the kind you're *supposed to feel* and you have to outlast it so when the time comes, if it comes, you get to see if you have what it takes to join the club.

He remembered a January morning, just before he went off to grad school. He watched the sun rise, doped the wind, and second guessed the placement of the decoys. But most of all, he remembered his beloved companion, Ogre, who sat with him on the bench watching the sky and sniffing the breeze. He was a massive chocolate coil of muscle and instinct locked for launch with only the very tip of his tail showing any sign of excitement. Sometimes he would grunt and sneeze as if to say, "Hey guys, you're missing something."

"Good boy, Ogre. Where are they? There!" John leaned forward and put his right hand on the gun. *Wait...wait...OK!* He stood, leveled the Browning, and fired.

✣ ✣ ✣

The son-in-law carted in with his goose.

"Sorry it took so long. They get the birds with a boat. There isn't a dog on the entire place."

"I know. It's not natural. Nice bird. How'd that old cannon do?"

"It jammed just like you said it would, but I only needed the one shell."

"I'll bet you were cold."

"They have heated seats in the blind. I'll take care of the bill and get the bird done. Then we can head home."

"Sure, sure…You drive us home, Bobby. I'm feeling a little stiff."

"Sure thing, Pop. I'll bring up the car."

"No hurry." John sat on the bench by the boxwoods and unzipped his coat.

✛ ✛ ✛

For a few fleeting moments, John was fifteen and frigid, as cold as he ever had been, and it got worse with every second as he struggled to get the decoys out before sun up. There was a skim of ice in the cove that had to go before the deeks could be set. His waders stuck in the muddy bottom, and he had to wrench each step free as he cast about, slapping the ice with an old paddle.

He was exhausted when he finally loaded his gun and slumped back in the blind. He watched dawn break over the water and thought about the ghost of Hamlet's father who describes first light as a glowworm, "Brief let me be." There was no wind, just silence. Ogre licked his chops and cocked his head.

"Where is it?" A tiny black dot shot toward the blind so low that its wingtips tapped the water leaving a wake of rings that extended back into the predawn shadows. It came at rocket speed, but the boy remembered the advice of the masters. *Lead twice what you think and then double it.* His first shot patterned inches behind the bird, but he was swinging the shotgun smoothly, and the second shell tumbled the drake.

Ogre casually waded into the water and did his swim-and-snort rhythm to the bird and back. He kindly shook off before entering the blind to drop the mallard at his master's feet.

✦ ✦ ✦

Bobby brought up the car, and the spell was broken. "You ready?"

✦ ✦ ✦

Back in the bar, the clipboard man said, "So who *was* that guy?"

"Haven't you seen the picture in the dining room? The tall guy and the dog? His people owned this land for generations, but for some reason, he sold it twenty years ago. He just pulled out. All that history, gone for good."

"That was him? Do you think he misses this?"

"This? No geese, tacky decorations…I don't know why he would."

"Yeah. He must have gotten cold feet."

"AWG" VERSUS HOG:

Meadow Lane, 1990

THE STEYR AUG AND A PILE OF ITS VICTIMS

I have been waiting for the world to collapse for forty years. When I first got into guns on my own, the assault-weapons craze was on full bore. Reagan was in the White House, and the Russians weren't having it. Nuclear war was just a matter of time. It seems ludicrous to say it now, but post apocalypse we figured that we would actually have to fend off surviving marauders. Nowadays, I am concerned about manmade disasters, such as a dirty bomb or biological attack in our cities that could create millions of refugees who are at wit's end about how to survive. The possibility doesn't keep me up nights. But while I am waiting around for things to get critical, I wonder what the combat rifle I bought can really do, and shooting it on the rifle range just doesn't count. Thank goodness for the groundhog, the ultimate pop-up target.

These animals are not stupid. Miss one once, and it will be forever wary. They can see you from a mile off. The king of groundhogs on my farm lived in a hole that ran right under our road, a problem that couldn't be ignored. Every time I got near him though, he buttoned up, and I had to choke on it. It got so bad that I never went out that gate without something that shoots.

Let me tell you, if you are using an ultra-short bullpup combat rifle from the driver's seat in a car, there are a couple of extra things to keep in mind.

I was in my wife's Chevy Nova with my window down. It was really early in the morning, and the grass was still wet. I silently coasted down the lane and stopped where I had the best view of the little plain that Mr. Chucky called his kingdom. The grass was a bit high, and we didn't see each other at first. Then he stood up. I know his little groundhog instincts told him to freeze. But he was smart, and even though he had to run almost straight at me, he bolted for his hole.

The AUG's scope has a big, black donut reticle that is perfect for this sort of thing, and I tracked him running left to right. He got to the edge of his hole, and I was as cranked over a far as I could get. He froze, and I pulled the trigger. The .223-caliber SX bullet didn't have far to go to hit something. You see, the AUG's scope sits several inches above the bore, and though I could see the target clearly in my fine Austrian optic, I could not see that the AUG's muzzle was pressed to the middle of the driver's side rearview mirror.

Of course the muzzle blast was deafening, and pieces of mirror, metal, and the fiberglass housing shot back at me. The rifle itself protected me from the shards. The mirror looked like something took a huge bite out of it, leaving the edges like the crust on a sandwich. I had some explaining to do. I don't think I told the truth about it at the time.

So this is my confession, and I will tell you what I learned:

Bullpup rifles are short, and so is my wife's temper. And King Groundhog? The bullet disintegrated on impact with the mirror, but he decided to move out anyway.

ONE FOR KITTY

Deer Park Inn

Buckhannon, WV, November 1995

A uthor's note: A feral cat is a wild animal. It can carry diseases, including rabies and a parasite called toxoplasmosis that can be very dangerous to humans with weakened immune systems. If you find yourself up against one of these animals, be very careful and seek professional help on how to handle it. If bitten or scratched by a feral cat, see a doctor immediately.

✝ ✝ ✝

I have only killed one animal in self-defense. It didn't attack me directly, but it came dangerously close to killing everyone in the house. This all took place way out in the country at my parent's bed and breakfast, the Deer Park Inn. This insidious interloper climbed through a small hole in the foundation of the lodge. Once under the house, it somehow managed to disconnect a rubber hose that fed natural gas to a fireplace. Luckily, an alarm sounded before anyone could fire up a cigarette. We shut off the gas, aired the place out, and then I had to crawl through the rats and copperheads to fix the problem.

That's when I met Bad Kitty.

I heard it hiss before I could see it, and I knew at once that I was dealing with a feral cat. Sure enough, it was a large, gray tuft of matted hair and wild instinct. It was large enough to give a raccoon a run for its money, and even with heavy gloves there was no way that I was going to touch it. I backed out and placed a Have a Heart Trap at the entrance of the crawl space. I baited it with sardines and waited until the following morning. I managed to catch a rat, but no cat. In fact, every time I set the trap, I wound up catching something unintended. This included chipmunks, a squirrel and a opossum.

The cat was on to us anyway, and it found several new ploys to piss us off. As I mentioned, my parents were running a bed and breakfast, and our customers loved everything about the place except for the cat paw prints all over their cars. Kitty also liked to howl at night. The guests' comment cards universally advised an end to Kitty's influence.

We decided that the cat simply had to go...so we loaded up our rifles and waited for a chance to take a clear shot. You would think that this gray marauder would quickly be dispatched, but it had a way of appearing only when standing in front of a car or a house. Every time we tried to get a clean shot, it anticipated our strategy and disappeared. This went on for weeks.

So, it was early November at Deer Park, and the leaves were at their height of beauty. We were already having a strange weekend. My oldest son had just turned four, and my mom threw him a little birthday party. She invited some of the locals, people we had never met, to bring their children out to Deer Park for balloons, a rousing game of pin the tail on the donkey, and cake. The kids were happily playing in the living room. I was chatting away with one of the parents when I happened to look out the window, and there sat Kitty without anything important behind him.

I called to my stepfather, "There's the cat! He's in the clear!"

"Get your gun!"

I ran for my .22, but my deer rifle was closer. The kids were shuttled into the dining room next door. I cracked the front door and tried to draw a bead, but it heard me and took a few steps that blocked my angle.

I wasn't going to let go.

"We need to shoot from the dining room entrance. Get the kids back in this room quick!"

The kids knew something was up, and their parents looked a little worried. I was oblivious to their reactions as I put the twenty-power cross hairs on the maddening target and pulled the trigger. I used a .243. I shot kitty with a seventy-grain SX bullet that is normally reserved for groundhogs and coyotes. The bullet is just barely stable and explodes on impact. I can only describe the effect in this instance as spectacular.

My stepfather and I went wild with excitement. We high fived each other a few times before I turned to where I thought our guests should be. As it turned out, we forgot to close the original door. The parents, their children, and my little birthday boy were drawn to the open portal, so they had an accidental front-row seat for the sanction.

The children looked confused. Forrest didn't bat an eye. He turned to his new friends and said, "Bye-bye bad kitty."

Our guests were speechless. How does one explain to four-year-olds that some of God's little creatures are pure evil?

We didn't even try. We just went straight to the cake.

KNIFE SEASON

Meadow Lane Farm, August 1976

One of the difficult things about growing up on the farm was reconciling my father's endless "when I was a kid stories" with reality as I knew it. I desperately wanted to experience that old-world excess. But times changed, and there was no longer any tolerance for antitank gun fun or the simple joy of dynamiting beaver dams. It took a generation—I suppose it was inevitable—but ever so slowly, the rules of decorum crept in. By my day, the shooting free for all was mostly a thing of the past. We had to think about how much noise we made... especially when shooting at night.

Night hunts *were* a Hirsh family tradition. We had a jeep with good headlights and hundreds of acres of open fields where all manner of critters made their nocturnal rounds. The strategy was to drive slowly, sweeping the headlights back and forth as we searched for a tell tale reflection.

"There! Eyes. See 'em? Two, four, eight deer there to the left. Bedded down. Come left till I can get a good angle on the big one in the middle."

We generally brought three guns on a night shoot: A .22, .410 shotgun, and an M-1 carbine loaded to the gills with military red-nose tracers.

I was the keeper of the ammo locker, and by my count in 1976, Dad had about two hundred rounds of military-grade, .30-carbine tracers on neat, little stripper clips. Today only two of these cartridges remain. Three of that lot are the basis for the story that follows. They are the only tracers I have ever fired, though I keep a bunch around, you know—for practical reasons.

So, I was fourteen and fascinated with Dad's guns. Hunting and shooting was our best common ground. His stories about watching tracers shot over his head in boot camp left me intensely curious about what a tracer looked like in action, but he was reluctant to shoot them without six inches of snow on the ground. It was summer, and I was wary of starting a forest fire. The national forest that surrounded the farm on three sides was a known tinderbox. In fact, I have an early memory of a major fire that threatened the farm. In addition to scores of professional firefighters, the state bussed in local high school students who had been trained in making fire breaks, but even that wasn't enough. Water-bombing aircraft made run after run, and thankfully we were mostly spared.

The entire event made a rather lasting impression on me, but I *really* wanted to see a tracer go. In my little pea brain, I figured that it would be perfectly safe to shoot one of the red tips into the river. I might have gotten away with popping one into the mighty Mississippi, but the Jackson is at best only four feet deep. It never occurred to me that the millionths of a second between the bullet's launch and hitting bottom was not enough time to observe the trace.

As it turned out, however, I had plenty of time to watch one fly. My "safe shot" hit a buried river rock and came straight back at me only a millimeter off its original line. The bullet actually grazed my right ear. I whipped around to see the blazing, red dot spiral wildly upward and then corkscrew down into the heart of the national forest.

I waited in a state of supreme angst for a forest fire, but it never happened. Now, you might think that I would learn something from this near-death/manmade disaster, but only weeks later I used our carbine to kill my first deer, a nice buck, in the middle of the night. I had a coconspirator, my wheel man, in the person of my grandfather's chef.

Back in those days, Pop had a restaurant called the Waterwheel, which offered five-star dining for the local fat cats and those guests at the Homestead resort who wanted a change in the menu. Pop did all the cooking for quite a while, but eventually he decided to bring in a promising young chef from New York.

Michael looked the part in the traditional headgear, and he was deemed quite lucky to have gotten such a prestigious gig right out of chef school. In fact, the New Yorker was bored to tears in Hot Springs, Virginia. He had heard quite a few stories about the Hirsh clan, and he jumped at the chance to go on a night hunt with me.

As it happened, I had been abandoned at the farm to spend some "quality time" with my grandparents. They paid absolutely no attention to my antics, so there was nobody around to say, "What the hell are you doing with that automatic rifle?" Or, "What the hell were you shooting at two in the morning?"

Up to this point, I had never hunted at night without my dad. I knew the strategy and the ground. I felt confident enough to solo. We did have a slight issue with transportation. We had always used our old jeep for the task, but Pop had traded it for a new Ford Bronco. It was the only four-wheel drive on the place so, naturally, we had to borrow it.

It was well after midnight when we launched our caper. I felt a certain exhilaration in sneaking off with the new truck. We silently coasted by the main house on our way down to the bottom fields. When we thought ourselves out of ear shot, we rumbled the engine and began our serpentine prowl of the killing fields.

We were out in the middle of the largest field, and there was a low mist that reduced visibility. Somehow, without noticing, we waded into a flock of does that remained frozen all around us. They were safe. The two bucks, eyes aglow in our high beams, were not.

Here we go. Get the gun up. Safety off. I shook violently with buck fever. *Finally, I get to kill something big.* I leaned out the passenger-side window. *This is just how you're supposed to do it. Get a rest on the mirror. I'm living the legend. Squeeze the trigger.*

I centered the front sight post on the left deer's chest and fired several times. The tracers had just enough space to really light up. Michael said that he could see the rounds pass through the target. The buck ran a few yards and dropped dead right in the middle of the jeep trail.

That's when the sinking sensation started.

I had not thought the entire action through, as there was no plan for disposing of a bullet riddled deer. I don't know how, but we got the body into the back of the Bronco and drove it out to a part of the farm we call "Airport Road."

Once upon time, we had a small plane and an airstrip, but my father wrecked the aircraft in a landing accident. The field had a boggy end, and Dad literally stuck the landing. My great-aunt, whose husband owned the plane, was thrilled to hear that the plane was down for good and better still, even though the engine was knocked back into the pilot's seat, and there was fuel everywhere, nobody was hurt. After that, our "airport" was allowed to revert to its primal state. The entrance was much overgrown. Not even the Bronco could penetrate it far. We tossed the stiff over the embankment. It rolled about twenty feet before it hit a log and came to a rest with its white belly shining skyward like a surrender flag.

Michael looked worried. "Do you think anyone would actually come out this road?"

I said, "Not without a good reason."

"Will the buzzards attract attention?"

Oh my God...I forgot about the buzzards. The sinking sensation took an even deeper plunge. By morning they would circle over the carcass in their hundreds, no doubt pointing out exactly where the poor victim was thrown. Pop would wonder what attracted so many birds. There might be an investigation. I could just hear the farm manager. "Mr. Hirsh...I took a look. There's a dead buck out there. It looks like it's been shot about fifty times. Who do you suppose killed it?"

Our cover-up went from bad to worse. There was a great deal of blood and hair in the nooks and crannies of the Bronco's tailgate. We drove it up to the barns for decontamination. It took some serious doing, but we managed to leave the back end of an otherwise mud covered Ford looking showroom clean. (Nothing screams cover-up like a half-sterilized truck.)

I left the farm the following day. My mother and stepfather picked me up, and we went on a road trip to South Carolina. But even in the getaway, I was still completely preoccupied with getting caught. Again, the way I figured it, based on epic stories that my father told me and countless gun blazing ride alongs, cool people ran around and shot anything that moved. You were supposed to make spectacular shots and brag about them to other like-minded individuals. Guns were revered, and most of all, because we owned the land, legal or not, it was open season on everything three hundred sixty-five days and nights a year. From the smallest green-eared slider terrapin to the mighty white-tail buck, nothing was safe.

All I wanted was a chance to make my bones and join their club. They had unintentionally groomed me for the purpose. After all, they taught me how to shoot very well. I was praised for my skills. I was trusted with a .22 magnum, and I roamed the farm with it for years. I was thoughtful about taking only the safest of shots. Groundhogs were my primary target, though anything else that hippy-hopped across my path was likely to take one from my Anchutz bolt-action rifle.

I first shot the M-1 carbine in December 1975. It was a few degrees below zero, and the ponds were frozen over. We carefully walked out into the middle of a wetland we call the "Slew." Dad handed me the little Winchester and said, "Shoot some holes so we can see how thick the ice is." I popped off a quick burst. Icy geysers sprayed upward, and I was sold on the little semi. After that I toted the carbine everywhere. I remember my first victim. I shot a muskrat with it, but I made the mistake of telling Pop. I thought he would be happy to know a much-detested animal was cleared out of the trout pond.

Nope. Pop unloaded on me. "You sit down, mister. You better listen to me or else! You better straighten up and fly right." There was that damn double standard again. He could laugh at the recounting of my dad's antics, even the shooting stuff, but when I pulled a similar stunt, he would explode on me. Let me tell you... he was never content with a simple "learn-your-lesson" correction. He wanted to see me cry and shrink in fear of his wrath. He had been doing this to me more or less continuously since I was four years old. Honestly, I think a great many animals died as sacrifices to the gods of teenage frustration, shame, and anger.

Anyway, we hadn't been in South Carolina long before guilt and anxiety over the dead buck completely overwhelmed me. I couldn't sleep or eat, and finally, I just went to pieces. I heard Pop in my mind. He was calling me names again. "You're an asshole, and a thoughtless, worthless killer." I realize now that I was punishing myself far beyond reason.

Nobody cared about poaching in 1970s Bath County, but I took no strength from such a reality check. The shame and remorse reached a crescendo that literally dropped me in my tracks.

Today we would call my reaction Post Traumatic Stress Disorder. There was no Xanax to give me relief. It was the kind of agony that burns out the hardwiring behind an otherwise well adjusted personality. Finally, I just had to lance the boil. I confessed to my mother.

She took my hands. "Hey, let me tell you something that might make you feel a little better. I am an accomplished night hunter myself. I never did the shooting, but I went along many, many times. Your father and his friends had this really stupid idea involving the jeep and these really long Randal knives they all had. One of them would stand on the truck's running board crouched over so he could stab at deer as they flashed by. They were going to call it Knife Season."

"How come Dad never told me about that?"

"Just for starters, it wasn't exactly a shining moment. They never actually connected with anything. Your father almost broke his neck one night chasing around like that. He also took a direct hit from a skunk. We had to scrub him down with tomato juice. Nobody got a Bloody Mary after church that Sunday. We tried to save the sweater, but we just couldn't quite get it totally de-skunked. Your father closed it up in a garbage sack and took it back to college with him. Then late one night he set the wooly stink bomb free in the office of a professor that he didn't like. That caused quite a stir. The professors were out for blood over it, but they had no idea who to accuse. Anyway, as for your caper, I don't think you need to worry about Pop finding out. You'll get away with it."

"I won't do it again."

"Oh, I bet you will. Just wait a few more years. And don't use the knife."

Mom was right on many levels. I never heard a thing about any obviously murdered whitetails. As it turned out, we picked a good spot to toss that poor buck. It took the buzzards and forest carnivores just a few hours to pick it clean. By the following evening, the place was quiet, and the deer were back.

Night hunting went out of fashion thirty years ago, but we still love to go for the after-midnight roll around to look for the odd fox, opossum, and deer. We have seen several black bear and bobcats. Our guests from New York City and Europe are always stunned by the sheer number of species that practically pose for pictures as we tool by in the dark.

Nowadays, only groundhogs and coyotes need live in fear. Deer are taken within the letter of the law. Nobody much bothers with small-game hunting. You can't swing a stick without jumping up a rabbit or fox squirrel. Red-tailed hawks, bald eagles, and osprey are everywhere and no doubt see our farm as an ideal hunting ground.

We still tell all those old stories, but somewhere along the line, the themes changed. The executioner's pride is long gone now. These days, we go for the "you won't believe this" recounting of past practices.

Now the next generation is up to bat. My sons are interested in hunting, but they wouldn't dream of shooting something at night or even out of season. Meadow Lane has become a sanctuary where survival of the fittest no longer includes competition with a knife wielding species or tracers in the night.

BAMBI'S NIGHTMARE

A Rural Middle School, 2000

Teaching in a small coal-mining town brings issues with postmodern textbooks into sharp relief. I found that our literature books offered endless subliminal messages that were in direct conflict with my rural students' values. Most texts are written for urban settings with urban sensibilities about world cultures. One issue in particular drove my students nuts—*animal rights*. Animal characters frequently thought like people; they even had hopes and dreams like humans. This use of anthropomorphic characters was a constant irritant.

Most of my students lived in the deep woods. Crocodile Dundee could get lost where these kids were from, and they were just about all hunters. Opening day of deer season was an unofficial school holiday. Killing a deer was an important right of passage both for boys and girls. You might find the blood-letting offensive, but their traditions get even more shocking. Twenty years ago kids brought guns to school all the time, not to shoot each other but to be used as props in demonstration speeches. They loved to give that gun-safety or how-to-clean-your-rifle lecture. Safe gun-handling skills were considered a universal sign of maturity and trustworthiness.

The rules about guns had been even looser a decade before my time at the school. Back then kids had to put their gun in a case before they *got on the school bus with it*. They had to *leave it in their locker* until their speech and put it back thereafter.

During my time, parents dropped off the gun, where it resided in the principal's office until the speech. I have to stress that in this community, guns must be considered in a different light. There is a reverence for their role and a pride in ownership that doesn't make much sense to people who live outside their neck of the woods. Gun ownership, like global warming, is often reduced to a matter of personal observation.

Then we have the suburban and city kids. Nearly seventy percent of all urban students populate a vastly diverse amalgam of cultural minorities, and more than half of these students are eligible for free or reduced-price lunch. Textbooks are written for this huge audience. Get this: New York City Public Schools and the Los Angeles Unified School District, the two largest in the county, each provide services to more students than the sum of all the students in twenty states. There are counties on Long Island that have larger enrollments than all of the students in West Virginia. My coal miners' kids' impressions just don't make the textbook editor's radar.

In the story, "The Dogs Could Teach Me" by Gary Paulsen, the narrator is a hunter/trapper in Alaska. As the title suggests, the story revolves around two of his sled dogs named Olaf and Columbia. Each dog had his own house and chain that kept him from reaching and fighting with his pack mates. The trapper observes Colombia, the smartest dog and leader of the team, place his bone just barely out of Olaf's reach.

"Columbia had measured it to the millimeter." The less intelligent team mate goes half insane trying to reach it. The smarter canine, "sat back and watched Olaf straining and pushing and fighting. Columbia leaned back and laughed. Heh, heh, heh...Then Colombia walked away." From this, the author infers that one dog had played a joke on the other. He then experienced a life changing assignation and says: "If a dog could [think like a human] then a wolf could do that, then a deer could that. If a deer could do that, then a beaver and a squirrel and a bird, and, and, and...I quit trapping then. It was wrong for me to kill."[1]

I know something about dogs. I have hunted with them all my life. My first job was working for a man who trained dogs for the DEA. I told my students about my experience with man's best friend. Rover may be domesticated, but he thinks like a dog, not a human. Dogs want to get the "reward item" and keep it. They want territory. Their first sense is smell. At best, the Einstein of dogs has the equivalent mental and emotional capability of a two-year-old. My students agreed.

---

1. Gary Paulsen. "In Trouble," in *Elements of Literature, Second Course*, 250–258. New York: Holt, Rinehart, and Winston, 2007.

Accompanying this tricky dog story is an inspirational essay about the Iditarod, an Alaskan dog-sled race, and the first woman to win the over one-thousand-mile trek. The kids are always suitably impressed, and there is a vital inference about the equality of the sexes that makes this story, in my mind, a must do. Unfortunately, my rural students sneer at it because of a single paragraph where the author relates that occasionally a moose will attack a musher, and it is a sad but necessary issue of self defense that the beast be killed. Apparently way up in Alaska there are moral rules about such things and the person who *has to* do the killing also has to skin the moose and bury it!

Hands shoot into the air. First, the kids ask how long this will take as there is a race going on. Second, they want to know how a 125-pound woman is going to move a three-hundred-pound moose. Third, why skin it? The extra weight on the sled would doom her chances of winning the race. Fourth, how'd she dig a hole in the frozen ground? It would also have to be one heck of a big hole. Fifth, isn't she just depriving the wolves of a free meal by burying it?

Geography makes a difference. City kids get a different message from this story. They infer that killing an animal in self-defense is a hassle to be avoided. Hunting, however, is simply out of the question. Without a frame of reference, the message goes unchallenged. When was the last time the average city student took a walk in the woods? My country kids were suspicious of every textbook story they read about animals after that.

They were positively influenced by one animal rights oriented story. "Let Me Hear You Whisper" features a cruelly treated dolphin that is used for scientific experiments. The bad-guy scientists try to make it speak, but to no avail. The dolphin knows that it is doomed if it doesn't talk, but steadfastly, bravely, it refuses to say anything to the white coats…but it *will speak* to the cleaning lady when nobody else is around. She shows pity for the imprisoned king of the sea. The climax comes when Flipper says softly, the word we've been waiting for: "Love."

For the record, I was for a while there, a member of Green Peace, but that, as they say, was back in the day, and I was studying marine biology at boarding school. The Green Movement had not swept into our consciousness. I learned a great deal about cetaceans (whales and dolphins). I like to sprinkle a little science into the lesson, and we cover their amazing brains, mammalian biology, and their behavior both in the wild and captivity. We discuss the morality of Sea World situations where these highly intelligent creatures go stir-crazy...oops, I let my bias show. The kids then write position statements, science reports, news stories, and ultimately creative essays about nature as they wish to interpret it.

I spent a lot of time in the field with my students and their families. I had several very successful groundhog hunts where my .22 Hornet came in handy. We chased after turkey, deer, squirrels, and the odd rabbit or two. I did some shot gunning with one of my students who was a champion West Virginia State trap shooter. Several of the teachers I worked with were avid shooters, and we did the gun-show circuit all the time.

1999: HAPPY HUNTING WITH ONE OF MY STUDENTS. THIS KID WAS A CHAMPION AIR-GUN SHOOTER WHO WAS ON HIS WAY TO JOINING THE WEST VIRGINIA UNIVERSITY RIFLE TEAM.

There were one or two odd gun related moments. Waaayyyy back there in 1989, I had a seventh grader bring in an interesting item for me to check out. We were standing in our bus lines, ready to go home. One of my all time favorite students, I'll call him Jimmy, called me over.

"Hey, Mr. Hirsh! Do you know what this is?" He handed me a metal tube, and I recognized its real identity instantly.

"What are you doing with an M-16's bolt carrier? This is for the fully automatic version, the real thing. It's restricted."

"I thought that I would stump you on this one! It belongs to my dad."

"Good Lord! Take it home. I don't want to know." The idea that the kid probably had access to a machinegun didn't bother me, but I called his father anyway.

Jimmy was good at shocking people. He was a less than organized student, and I was always inspecting his locker to make sure he wasn't creating a health hazard or stealing other kids' textbooks.

Each student had a locker with two sections. The bottom was for coats and the top was for texts.

"Ok, Jimmy, let's see how your locker is holding up."

"Sure thing Mr. Hirsh."

The locker was all neat and tidy down below, but it was the porno magazine cover he had propped up to face out so boldly that caught and kept my attention. I didn't want to stare at it for too long, but it was some really hardcore stuff and I was actually a little stunned. Eventually, I laughed and deposited the offending parchment in a manila envelope. We went down to the office, and I gave the evidence to the principal who was also amused about the whole incident.

Apparently Jimmy was let off with a warning. I thought he would be mad at me for turning him in, but he never stopped smiling, particularly after I told him that I saw our principal carry that envelope out to his car.

The other gun oriented incident takes the cake.

I used to build the sets for school plays. One of my workers, a senior, brought in a load of lumber, and as we were unloading it, I asked if he had the nails we asked for. He said, "Yes, look behind the seat under the shotgun shells."

He had a Mossberg twelve-gauge, pump-action shotgun that obviously lived there and must have been in his truck during the school day. It was squirrel season, and that was reason enough for me to shrug it off. It is important to note that all of these incidents occurred prior to passing the Gun Free School Zone Act.

I spent fourteen wonderful years at that school. During that time I lost nine students to car accidents and ATV disasters. Nine empty seats. We had no accidental shootings or gun crime. Yes, these families were heavily armed, and yes, a lot of game was taken. These kids experienced wildlife in a way that is quite unimaginable to kids who have never been to a summer camp in the country.

If you want to know something real about animals, these are the kids to consult. I recall one of our quarterbacks who made a lot of money raising calves for competitions. He was a big deal in FFA (Future Farmers of America). Oh, yes, my students raised all manner of farm animals, fowl of all sorts, dogs, cats, aquaculture, and don't forget the horses.

Students brought animals to school all the time. For example, I assigned my seventh graders to do a three-minute speech, with a visual aid, about something you do around the house. You could always go with making a sandwich or tying your shoes. Jimmy brought in a sheep that he was raising for FFA. He put it on my desk with its rear facing the audience and gave a how-to speech about an immanent surgical procedure.

The sheep was perfectly behaved, but let out one bleat that attracted our principal's attention. He was a good old boy at heart and laughed his ass off when he came into the room.

"Dr. Jones, believe it or not, I have a lesson plan for this."

"I'm sure you do, Phil. I love it. Can I stay?" he asked politely. Jimmy invited him right in. It was one of the best speeches of all time.

The worst part of this textbook-selection, cultural mismatch is the insinuation that he or she who kills an animal is just barely shy of committing murder. In my experience, the exposure to hunting and gun responsibility makes students all the more trustworthy.

THE THIRTY-FOURTH FLOOR

The Big City, Modern Day

Jane Brennen stepped into the elevator. She was tall and willowy with brown hair and a warm smile. She said hello to a fellow homeward bounder and shot out her hand to stop the door as another familiar face made a quick dash. The occupants didn't really know each other's stories. They came from a wide array of offices. Normally, these vertical commuters wouldn't give each other the time of day, but they were the famous few that spent three hours stuck between the twenty-seventh and twenty-eighth floors, a minor trauma that bonded them together.

Jane had no way of knowing for sure, but she thought it likely that she was the only one in the group who didn't grow up in the city. She was a country girl who came to town with a pocketful of scholarships and a serious work ethic. Jane hunted down a job at a five star restaurant and made great tips. She was utterly focused and graduated from the university with a 4.0 grade-point average and without a cent of debt.

Jane took an internship that became a full time job, and promotions came rapidly as the company blossomed. She was assertive but not unpleasant. Her boss said with a smile, "Don't ask Jane to do something unless you are really sure you want it done." The next thing Jane knew, there was a sizeable surplus in her bank account. After much deliberation, she paid cash for a new, in-box Remington Model 700 BDL bolt action hunting rifle—the fancy one with all the trimmings.

Jane Brennen was a serious deer hunter as the phone in her hand did attest.

32ᵗʰ Floor

"Thanks for holding the door. You're name is Jane, right? I'm Andrew."

"Yes, I remember now. No problem."

"Cool phone." Jane offered him a look.

"This is my new screen saver. It's my buck. I just got this picture from my dad. The taxidermist did an incredible job. I shot it at our farm in Missouri. Ten-point rack. I still can't believe it."

"And you're really happy about that?" The young man had a hostile tone.

Jane sensed trouble. "You tell me. Look at it! I'm not thrilled about the cost to have it mounted, though."

"Shooting that animal...you took a life...that deer should have the same right to live as we do. How could you do that?"

"With a rifle and sometimes a bow."

30ᵗʰ floor

Jane turned to another rider, "Here, what do you think?"

"Wow! Fine with me. Obviously you ate it, right."

"Not in one seating. We'll eat a deer like that in a week. We always give meat to friends, and we make giant vats of chili and spaghetti sauce, roasts, stir-fry meat, tenderloin, back straps, ribs…"

29ᵗʰ floor

"It's murder!" Andrew interjected.

"And jerky. Sounds good, doesn't it?"

Jane was surprised at the vociferous demonstration, and for the briefest of moments, she considered putting her phone away.

✢ ✢ ✢

Like all of the Brennens, Jane was an accomplished hunter and shooter. An only child, her mother died when she was very young, but her father protected and nurtured her through their mutual pain, and they emerged on the other side of grief devoted to each other and the land they called their family home. They spent a great deal of time at the barns working with their sheep, goats, and horses. It was good therapy.

They rode Hubcap and Trudy almost every day. Both horses knew the circuit that began in the woods and emerged onto two hundred acres of flat green grass. It was a natural shooting gallery, and the deer didn't seem to notice.

Jane's father dismounted and led Hubcap by his reins. "Look at this, Janie. Here's something you won't see on *Sesame Street*. Ready to hop down? Herewegooo. Now, see those? They are deer tracks. There's a lot you can tell from these tracks. You see how they are running right along this path? Deer are creatures of habit. They'll be back tomorrow, and all the days after until deer season when the biggest, best buck is going to be ours."

Little Janie added the lesson to her vast understanding of the natural world. She had no fear of snakes or spiders. She baited her own hooks and shook off the scrapes and cuts that come with farm work. There was nothing hiding under her bed unless it was one of her dogs. She loved school. Her fifth grade teacher, Mrs. Whitenight, told her that she was gifted. She, of course, was speaking of academics. Janie assumed it had something to do with the fact that she already knew how to drive farm trucks, mowers and the big tractor.

Janie learned to shoot all types of guns as well as the bow. She hunted squirrels and groundhogs from a very young age. She killed her first doe at eleven, and the following season she took her first buck. Her picture was in the local newspaper, and the clipping remained on the refrigerator for ten years. There were no tears about it, and absolutely no guilt. She was part of nature itself.

Janie presented a note to the school secretary.

> Please excuse Jane from class tomorrow. She will be deer hunting.

"Deer hunting again, Janie?"
"Yup! I'm a predator, but a nice one."
"Good luck. You be careful! Bring us a picture for the bulletin board."

✦ ✦ ✦

27th Floor

The lawyer for the animals' defense kept up his tirade. "The way you gut the poor things is nothing short of barbaric! No, that's too nice a word! It's depraved!"

Janie touched her phone's screen to summon up another picture. "You mean like this? Once I skin one, we let it hang in the cold which cures the meat."

"Oh! I'm going to be sick!" He managed a dry heave for the audience.

✦ ✦ ✦

Cleaning the deer was all very scientific. By middle school Janie, knife in hand, was up to her elbows in the process. She could identify all the major organs, bones and cuts of meat. Though only a child, Janie understood the power and responsibility of handling firearms because unlike most children, she had a chance to see the effect for herself.

Jane loved detective shows and fancied herself as a medical examiner. She always made observations about entry and exit wounds and the damaged organs in between. "Maybe I should be a vet. I could do an operation."

✣ ✣ ✣

25ᵗʰ Floor

"The need to kill is a sickness. There must be something missing in your life. And guns! Don't get me started on the gun insanity. Do you have an assault weapon?"

"Not really. Though I do pity the poor fool that breaks down my door."

✣ ✣ ✣

"Little girl," Janie's dad said, "You know your gun safely. I like the way you are so careful with your BB gun. Now it's time to learn about real-live rifles. As you know, a hunting rifle is an extension of yourself. You need to find one and stick with it. I've been faithful to my Winchester, and it has never let me down. You know that your mother gave me this gun. It's a part of me for lots of reasons that, oddly enough, have nothing to do with actually firing it. A stranger could pick it up and say it weighs eight pounds. He can't feel the family, pride, and tradition in it. He could look in a book and say what the rifle is worth, but you and I know a king's ransom wouldn't even come close."

Jane remembered the smile on her dad's face when she brought her new Remington in from the car.

"So you finally bought yourself your own gun." Her father chuckled. "Let's get it on our bench and see if it'll shoot."

Janie settled in behind her rifle. Sandbags held it absolutely still, and she allowed the barrel to cool between shots. She had faith in the .243 cartridge with one-hundred-grain soft point bullets, and fired a total of twenty rounds in the first session. She needed seven to zero the bargain priced 4-12 power scope. The other thirteen rounds revealed a few problems.

First, she had to give the scope a boot full of rudder to get it on paper, and though her groups were less than two inches, they were vertical strings, not healthy little triangles. Her last two shots went completely wild and blew the group to almost eight inches.

✛ ✛ ✛

24ᵗʰ Floor

"Do you support using lab animals for drug tests? They use monkeys, you know. They use rabbits to test your make-up."

"You've got the wrong girl. Do you see any make-up on this face?"

✛ ✛ ✛

The Brennen family's gunsmith was as trusted as their family doctor. Jane expressed her disappointment and frustration with her new rifle.

"Jane, why didn't you come to me with your problem sooner? I could have saved you a lot of time and money. You know how I feel about this brand of scope. Do you see any here in my store? Tell me the truth. Did they put the scope on at that damned rip-off market some people call a gun store?"

"Oh yes. That service came free with the gun. I should have just done it myself."

"You would have done a better job. Pathetic. These scope rings are crap. The base wasn't tightened down. I went over the scope mounts and rings and, gosh...I don't know how to say it...I accidentally broke your scope. I am very sorry. My bad. I installed a nice, used Leupold 3-9 power scope that I had lying around. I bore sighted it, glass bedded the action, and free floated the barrel except for a little glass pad at the tip of the channel. I tuned the trigger too. I think it's light enough to be good and heavy enough to be safe. I won't do trigger work for just anybody anymore. The liability is a real issue, and people are idiots."

Her gunsmith shook his head. "I know you expected better from Remington. They make fine guns. Times have changed. Manufacturers cut all kinds of corners. Some companies even sell their screwed up factory second rifles to mass merchants like the one where you found this rifle. Just about every firearm coming off the production lines, even some of the top shelf stuff, needs the final touches. This rifle will *really* shoot now, as you will soon see. You'll need shells."

"One-hundred-grain softies, please."

"You can trust these. Remember, never buy bullets at mass merchants. He pulled two boxes off the shelf. How's your dad?"

"Still shooting."

"Good. He's still got that .270 pre-64 Featherweight?"

"Sure does. I'll tell him you said hello to his gun."

1960. THE AUTHOR'S FATHER POSES WITH AN ANTELOPE HE TOOK WITH HIS THEN BRAND-NEW .270 MODEL 70 WINCHESTER. WE STILL USE IT TO THIS DAY.

20th Floor

"Andy...Andy!" Jane said. "You need to calm down, take a goddamn breath."

The suggestion just added to the fire.

✝ ✝ ✝

The deer on Janie's farm spent their nights grazing in the open field. As soon as the sun began to rise, they wandered back toward the woods. During rut, however, there was a party going on in that field until well after full light. The shot fired from their blind might fall anywhere from fifty all the way out to almost four hundred paces.

Jane sighted in her rifle for "maximum point-blank range." She knew how to use ballistics tables. At a hundred yards, her bullets printed about four inches high, but at three hundred yards, the bullet's arch was back to flat on. So long as she held her sights at the base of the deer's heart, a hit between the aorta and the bottom of the chest cavity would lay the deer low.

✝ ✝ ✝

19th -3rd floor

Jane's adversary rambled about his devotion to PETA. He upped the ante. Owning dogs, cats, and even fish amounted to slavery. Janie countered with the universal "stop-right-there-and-tell-it-to-the-hand" gesture.

"*Oh hell no*...Enough, Andy! If you don't like hunting that's fine, that doesn't bother me. Everybody is entitled to an opinion. BUT, you can keep your accusations to yourself there, *buddy*." She jabbed a finger in his chest. The elevator was tight, but the commuters found room to move back and give the contestants a clear field. Andy obviously felt well armed with insinuation and guilt. His opponent wielded biology and the game laws.

The animal advocate tried to filibuster and looked for a quick exit. The elevator opened several times, but Jane kept hitting the door-close button.

"We're full," she announced. Then she turned back to her opponent. "You aren't getting out of here so easy."

✦ ✦ ✦

The buck immortalized in Jane's phone tried to sneak across the field at almost three hundred yards. He chased two does that crossed before him. Jane put her anticipation in check and focused her senses.

Let the rifle naturally point and move your body to align the gun. Let the breathing slow. Consider the distance and note any wind.

She didn't have much time. The buck was moving and could bolt at any moment. Another doe appeared, and he investigated. They danced and shuffled, paused and sprinted. Jane collected the slack in the trigger and held the .243 at three and a half of the four pounds needed to drop the firing pin. The dancing ungulates paused, smelling something they didn't like. *Recalculate.* The white tails went up. *Now.* Jane's bullet rang out. She heard the thud echo as it hit home.

The buck reared, kicked, and fell in a heap.

A little voice thundered, "Good shot, Mommy! You got 'em! Let's go see! Let's go see!" Jane's seven-year-old still had her ear defenders on. She was wrapped up in a blaze-orange hoody that came to her ankles.

Jane took her daughter's earphones off. "You don't have to yell, sweetie. That's how we hunt. High five! Low five! If you like, you can try it someday. You were very good to be so quiet."

"And I'm your spotter. I saw him first."

"Yes you did eagle eye. Let's go get Grandpa. We're going to need the truck."

"Oh! I want to drive. Can we live here?"

"Let's see what Daddy thinks when he gets back from his job in Iraq."

"I can spot for him, too."

"He will love that."

✢ ✢ ✢

2ⁿᵈ floor

The elevator doors opened at the mezzanine, and with a huff, the animal-rights man made his exit. When the doors closed everyone snickered.

"Good Lord!" said the man in the Italian suit.

"You go, girl!" said the white-haired lady. She added a friendly squeeze of her arm.

"Yeah! Girls and guns, am I right?" the intern offered.

"Damn straight!" Jane said to all.

"I know which office he works in if you'd like me to deliver some jerky."

"Nice thought but that won't leave any for the rest of us! Same time tomorrow?"

The Lobby

The car pool dispersed with many the pleasantry.

"I'm Chris, by the way. See ya, Jane."

"Sure, see you later."

"I'm Tia. Have a good night, Jane."

"What do you drink with jerky?" asked Mr. Italia.

Sylvia waited for the others to drift away. She produced a cigarette and prepared to light it. "I'll check to see if jerky is kosher, but on the other hand, I could make an exception!"

"Oh, OK, I guess..."

"See you sweetie. I feel sorry for that Andrew...a little. Actually very little...if at all. Ha! Bye now!"

Jane gave a little wave. She paused and caught her breath. Her heart rate slowed, and her anger subsided. She looked at her screen saver again and did a quick gut check. Yes, she still felt only pride.

THE ARBALETE

Saint Croix, 1959–1962

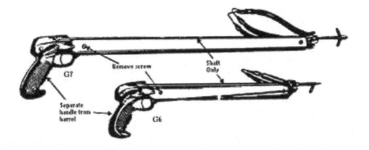

Abercrombie and Fitch was at one time the premier, one-stop shop for wealthy sportsmen. No matter what the quarry, from New England whitetail deer to African lions, Abercrombie had the tools and tack for any hunting adventure. Fishermen found their paradise on the store's seventh floor. Freshwater anglers could select from a goodly number of the finest handmade bamboo poles, but saltwater fishermen had an unparalleled array of equipment that could land everything from a sailfish to a great white shark. Best of all, Abercrombie had all that the intrepid sportsman needs to catch deep sea Titans without a pole or even a hook.

They sold the Arbalete spear gun—the finest underwater weapon then in existence. Its power came from double, surgical-hose elastic bands that were stretched to their absolute limit and held by a trigger just like any gun. Spear fishing was a popular sport in those days, and there were no rules about what was fair game in the water. The fish had one advantage. Normally, skin divers have only seconds on the bottom to find and fire at a target, but bottled air made the scene and the kill rate increased dramatically.

The *Self-Contained Underwater Breathing Apparatus* was by no means common in the late 1950s, and the early models lacked the safety features that make modern scuba diving relatively safe. There were no diving classes where a novice could learn about the dangers of the bends or nitrogen narcosis. Nor were there many destinations where one could have his air tanks refilled, so Abercrombie delivered the equipment ready for use.

My father purchased the whole rig and had it sent to the Buccaneer Hotel in Saint Croix—a home away from home for the Hirsh family. He slipped down to the island by himself during spring break at Yale to play with his new toys.

The story always begins with the same invocation: "I blame Walt Disney for everything that happened. We all had seen the movie *20,000 Leagues under the Sea,* and we were keen to visit that world for ourselves. It was filmed in Jamaica off the Negril Beach.

"I went there with father in 1955, long before there was anything on that stretch of beech but coconuts. It's like Disneyworld now. We wanted to see where they filmed the movie and confidently went into the water and swam out. Trouble was, the water was cloudy, and we had no luck finding any of the stuff they left behind. It got really spooky when the bottom dropped off, and it became more and more difficult to see anything. Then there were the remoras, lots of them, and they seemed to think that we were sharks as they appeared to be trying to attach themselves to us. That did it. Remoras plus cloudy water equals sharks in the area, invisible in the gloom. It was a long swim back to the beach and the remoras didn't stop chasing us until we were able to stand up. We decided right there that only a lunatic would go out in those waters without some means of defending himself.

"As for sport, all those years ago, there was no shortage of fish to spear. My prey of choice included grouper and lobster, but on my first dive with a scuba tank, I took on a deep-sea monster that anyone with even the least amount of common sense would have left well enough alone.

"I hired a boat to take me out into the middle of the harbor, which was about one hundred feet deep. I was alone, a cardinal foul in the scuba-diving rule book, and I had no idea that I was literally daring death to swim up behind me and take me to the bottom."

Once in the water, Dad adjusted his mask, cleared his mouthpiece, and scanned the underwater world. He was an experienced skin diver who could hold his breath for more than a minute. It was nothing for him to dive fifty feet or more without the slightest exertion. So when freed from the one breath approach, but on the clock with only fifteen minutes of air, he followed his old habits and shot straight for the bottom.

"I had no idea that you were supposed to descend gradually and, more importantly, that you have to decompress as you come back up. I was overwhelmed by the beauty all around me. My scuba tank allowed me to savor the scene. The water was warm and absolutely clear. I was enveloped by schools of small fish. The sea anemones were in full bloom, and the coral teemed with life that covered every color and description. Moray eels watched me swim by. Reef sharks and bands of barracuda gave me the once-over. But I was used to their presence, and I wasn't out to shoot them anyway."

He chased a lobster for several minutes, but it scurried beneath the fire coral before he could get off a shot. Even with the Arbalete, a spear fisherman had to get close. The weapon's range was only twelve feet, and the spear itself was attached to the gun by a stout line. A lanyard loop around the wrist ensured that the diver did not lose his weapon if the speared fish tried to escape.

"I misjudged this range only one time, and that was while Kyle and I were on the beach prepping for a dive. I was frustrated by a series of missed shots and complained that I could do better with the Arbalete on land than in the water. Kyle laughed and yelled, 'There's a green monster right behind you!' I knew that he was referring to the Volkswagen we had rented, and I thought that I was definitely more than twelve feet from the car. I wheeled around in my best James Bond, man-of-action mode and let fly. As it turned out, I was eleven feet six inches away from the car. The spear went right through the door."

On the first dive, however, my father had no real appreciation for what his spear gun could and could not do. "I had total faith in the double 'rubbers,' which were said to offer the mightiest of whacks to anything one cared to skewer. As I ascended, with less than a minute of air left, I encountered a target that I could not resist shooting.

"I was still down about sixty feet when a school of massive tarpon went by. There were about a hundred of them, none less than six feet long, and I could practically touch them. There was one particularly huge fish bringing up the rear, and I thought why not just shoot 'em in the head and drag him up to the boat."

Dad used his duck hunter instincts to lead the torpedo of a target. The spear rapidly slows as it goes, and by the time it hit the fish it was out of oomph and simply bounced off the tarpon's legendary, tough scales.

"I could actually hear the spear hit, but the tarpon itself didn't even seem to notice. I had no knife with me to cut the wrist lanyard. If that spear had somehow found a chink in that armor and the spear's snelled point got a good grip, I would have been dragged out to sea and drowned for sure. It was the single luckiest simultaneous hit-and-miss of all time."

There were other subsurface close calls. Years later, while on a family trip to Bermuda, my father's scuba tank gas-regulator system failed. Our hotel was right on the beach, and divers could wade right out to explore the lagoon. I was five years old, and I recall vividly what happened after he came out of the surf.

My mother said, "Look. Here comes daddy back from the deep!" I watched him strip off his gear and drop it on the sand as he came toward us. I thought he was throwing it all away. He came to our table and sat down. He had this strange look in his eyes, as if he were blind to us. My mother asked him what was wrong. First he demanded to know who "the hell" we were. Then he became furious and slammed his hands on the table, threw back his chair, and stormed off toward the hotel.

I might have been in preschool, but I knew that something must have gone wrong on the dive. Mom chased after him, but by the time she reached the lobby, he was gone and nowhere to be found. As it turned out, he went to the first open door he found and into someone else's room. He took off his swimsuit, threw it out into hall, closed the door, and collapsed out cold on the bed. By this point the entire staff was looking for Dr. Hirsh who was clearly suffering from nitrogen narcosis. Their only clue to his whereabouts was a soggy swimsuit. The search went on for more than a hour before a maid found him—safe, sound, and stark naked—when she entered the room to turn down the bed.

There was a serious investigation as to how the hotel-provided equipment had malfunctioned. "It was CO^2 that got me. There was a pin hole in the diaphragm of the regulator, so I was breathing air way to polluted with CO^2."

My mother says that this near calamity was par for the course with my father who thought nothing of risking it all to have more fun. The first time this occurred was perhaps the most reckless incident of them all.

They were on their honeymoon and had rented a sailboat with a captain and crew to sail them around the region for two months. My mother recalls, I will never forget how our honeymoon started. Your father wanted to hear real Trinidad Jazz so we went to this whorehouse which was said to be the best place. I was too freaked out to enjoy the music. This was a common theme with your father in those days.

On their first scuba dive together, my parents explored the wreck of an Argentine supply ship that had been torpedoed by a submarine in 1944. It was carrying a shipload of bones that would have been ground up into fertilizer had it reached its destination. It sank on Anegada Reef in such a way as to leave about ten feet of the bow out of the water. The rest, more than two hundred feet of rusted and mangled steel, descended into the black at a forty-five degree angle.

I have heard the story from both points of view. Mom loves to tell it whenever the subject of ex-husbands comes up.

"It was a pretty picture for the first fifty feet or so. Just exquisite. The sunken wreck was home to what had to be thousands of fish. Coral grew all over the place, and there was not a barracuda or shark to be seen. I hadn't used a scuba tank before that trip, but I was raised in Florida by an avid deep-sea fisherman. And I was always pretty comfortable on the water, but your father fixed that.

"I followed my new husband as he went down the side of the wreck, but he saw a huge grouper and swam into the wreck to spear it. I just hovered outside. It took him a few minutes. But I could see his air bubbles coming up, and so I figured he was safe. I wasn't in the least bit worried.

"He chased the fish right out of there and shot it before it could get away. He was thinking that we were only seconds from the boat and the sharks wouldn't get the scent in time to come after us. The grouper was swirling around, still swimming and trying like mad to get back in the wreck."

My father recalls, "The damn thing was still alive, and it was leaking a blood-red cloud that obscured my view of the bottom until a half-dozen reef sharks broke through and came straight for my fish. Now, this was the biggest grouper I had ever shot—one for the record books—and I wasn't about to let it go. I had tangled with small sharks before, and I wasn't afraid of them. I could easily fend them off by poking at them with the business end of my Arbalete, but this time I had a raging grouper pulling at me for all it was worth and so no prod for my defense."

My mother remembers a little less adventure. "My idiot husband didn't let go of the damn fish, and more sharks came. I remember that they shot around both the sides of the wreck and came straight for me. I was terrified and nearly spit out the mouthpiece to scream. I swam for the surface and climbed out of the water on that rusty bow. I scraped myself on something and was bleeding, so I wasn't going back in that water.

"I thought, Honey, you are on your own! More and more sharks came, and a feeding frenzy began. There were fins sticking out of the water, racing around, and then I saw something really terrifying. It was a hammerhead shark. I watched my father land a ten-footer when I was a kid. For a split second, I thought, Oh my God, it's back, and my husband has no idea that it's between him and the boat."

Their captain realized the danger and maneuvered their launch to rescue his clients. He pulled right up to the wreck, but my mother still had to swim a short distance to reach the boat.

"Your father reached the surface with sharks all around him, and he was still dragging that bloody fish with him. I could see it all. I screamed a warning when the hammerhead slid by, not ten feet from me, and then it went straight for him. Thank goodness it veered to get the grouper. He kicked and punched at it. It turned away, but the rest of the black tips—some more than three or four feet long—were more determined than ever to take it from him. Then the hammerhead changed direction, rolled over, and barreled back in. I thought, Well, that's it. Two weeks, and I'm a widow.

"Your father made it to the speed boat, held up the grouper, and said something to the captain who was shouting frantically to just get rid of it, but your father is so damn stubborn that he didn't take that very sound advice. He handed his spear gun to the captain who reeled in the fish, cussing it all the way. Then your father did the strangest get get-out-of-the-water move I have ever seen. He faced the sharks and angled his body downward so that his fins were up in the air. The captain grabbed him by the ankles and pulled him out of the water as he thrashed at the sharks with his knife. Now that was knife season if ever there was one.

"I knew right then that our marriage wasn't going to last. Either he would get himself killed, or I would kill him. It was just a matter of time."

The Arbalete sat in the corner of my father's study for years after that. If the grouper/shark fest was a fair fight, than this last outing with it was about as unsporting as it gets. This time it was used on the Virginia shore where a friend of our family has a sprawling estate right on the water.

Back in those days, the Chesapeake Bay was still thriving. The waters had not been contaminated by fertilizer runoff from farms that dot the shore in all directions. We had a seine net that was more than one hundred feet long and eight feet deep. It had weights on the bottom and floats on top. We fed it off a rowboat in a huge semicircle with each end on the sandy beach. It took five people on each end and an intrepid swimmer in the water to duck under and free the net when it got hung up on any number of obstacles. We finally pulled it in and captured dozens of bass, which we carefully released. We kept the crabs and, above all, the huge carp, some weighing twenty pounds or more, for some rather eccentric fun.

There was a defunct swimming pool on the property filled with the bay's brackish water. This became the carps' new home, and they readily took to it. Then came the spear gun fun. At first they ran around the pool and fired the Arbalete from above the surface. They knew exactly how to compensate for refraction, but the carp lounged on the bottom out of range. Not to be deterred, they went in after them, but in the end, they only shot a few of the fish before they actually reconsidered what they were doing. I was somewhat surprised that they didn't kill them all because we considered them to be inedible trash feeders.

Kyle said, "Someone should take a picture of this and send it to the *American Sportsman* magazine."

Looking back, I would posit that this unusual clemency was the turning point in the lives of two sportsmen who had never known restraint above or below the waves. Twenty years mellowed their more vicious instincts. Rather than stick them, they named the fish and chased after them for a bit of carp wrestling. I think that they enjoyed their bizarre fish tank far more than any hunt.

I have no idea what happened to the Arbalete after that. Abercrombie and Fitch went out of business, and serious spear guns have been outlawed in the Caribbean.

The Arbalete stands out in my mind as one of the Hirsh clan's most important guns. It didn't roar and stomp like the antitank gun or spew bullets like the MP-44. It lacked the glamour of a silver six-gun. We could only imagine what these guns were like in actual combat. Playing with them didn't make you a soldier or the local sheriff. But the Arbalete was entirely different. Unlike any other weapon in our considerable arsenal, while we prowled under sea, this rubber-powered wonder made you Captain Nemo.

ABOUT THE AUTHOR:

Philip Reid Hirsh III has been a lead educator, rural schools specialist, and curriculum theorist for more than twenty-five years. He has an undergraduate degree in English from the University of Richmond and a master's degree in secondary education from the West Virginia University. He returned to WVU twenty-five years later to teach educational psychology and complete a doctorate in curriculum theory. Phil is a lifelong competitive marksman, gun broker, and hunter who uses his background in social research and storytelling to explore gun culture. He has two sons, Forrest, twenty-three, and Hunter, nineteen. He resides in Morgantown, West Virginia with Anne, his wife of twenty-six years and Zasu, their Springer spaniel.

Made in the USA
Columbia, SC
06 March 2018